Historic Ludwigstrasse Coloring Book

A brief tour of the vibrant, open-air, art museum that is the Lüftlmalerei of Garmisch-Partenkirchen in Bavaria, Germany

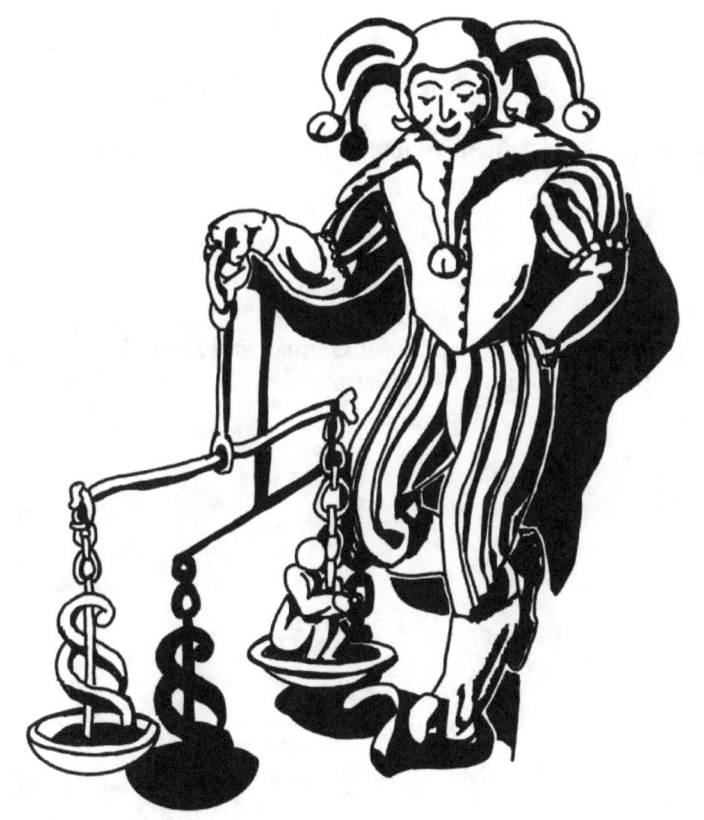

Justin Vazquez

For Olivia and Eli,

who have copied and colored doodles of staplers, cows, and flying saucers scribbled in the margins of birthday and holiday cards from me for years.

With special thanks to Paul Dutro,

whose guided tour of the town first inspired this particular publication,

and Franz Wörndle, town archivist,

who politely tolerated my attempts at German and allowed me to thumb through stacks and stacks of Garmisch-Partenkirchen's history.

Copyright © 2020 Justin Vazquez

https://lueftlmalerei.com

All rights reserved.

ISBN: 979-8-5768-3929-2

INTRODUCTION

When you think of Southern Germany, you likely picture King Ludwig's fairytale castle, Lederhosen, or Oktoberfest. But just as quintessentially Bavarian are the murals on the sides of homes, businesses, and even barns — scenes from the Bible, the lives of Saints, or just rustic, rural life.

In the town of Garmisch-Partenkirchen these outdoor wall paintings are called "*Lüftlmalerei.*" In German, "*Luft*" means "air," and "*Malerei*" means "painting," so "Lüftlmalerei" means an "airy" outdoor "painting."

This style of art can be traced back two thousand years, to the 1st century, when Romans decorated the walls of their estates with plaster and stucco. Dye and pigments were painted into the plaster while it was still wet, and when it dried, there was a waterproof and lasting "*fresco*" (Italian for "fresh") painting.

As Christianity spread from Rome north beyond the Alps, a cult of saints began to form. As their cults grew, saints' remains became relics – magical objects believed to be capable of performing miracles long after the saint had died — and saints' graves became places people would make special trips to see. Artists used the plaster fresco technique to paint on the walls of pilgrimage churches to tell the stories of the lives of saints.

While the style first spread as church decoration, it was quickly copied. Soon, throughout Germany, town halls, market stalls, and city walls were painted with images of important events, major battles, and the stories from the lives of kings. Gate towers were covered with an impressive reproduction of the cities' coat of arms on the shields of fearsome warriors. German legends were writ large across imposing castle walls. It wasn't long before well-to-do Germans began decorating their homes in the same way — just like the Romans had, a millennium before.

By the 18th century, just as fresco painting was falling out of fashion in the major cities, it began to take hold in the foothills of the Alps. Traders, warehouse owners, and craftsmen started to display their wealth on the walls of their homes. Religious motifs were still popular, but so were references to local, everyday life. Those who could afford to, could have their patron saint, or their family crest, or some simple slogans extolling the wisdom of rural life tattooed on the stucco walls of their simple *Hof*.

Alpine homes are perfect for this style of painting. The walls of Bavarian and Tyrolean farmhouses are almost always plastered white, providing an ample canvas for fresco painters to fill with bright, cheerful colors.

"Ludwigstraße," (German for "Ludwig's Street") in the town of Garmisch-Partenkirchen is named for Ludwig II, the Fairytale King, who built the Neuschwanstein castle and who often stayed overnight here on his way to his hunting lodge in the nearby mountains.

The shops and buildings on Ludwigstrasse have been covered with Lüftlmalerei for hundreds of years. If you walk down the street today, you might wonder, what do these particular paintings mean? Why are they here and what do they show? This picture book, like a walk down Ludwigstrasse, tells some of the stories of Garmisch-Partenkirchen, its people, and its place in history – a story written in its Lüftlmalerei.

As you put your own creative talents to work coloring these images, you can see what these paintings actually look like and learn about the artists who painted them by going online to https://lueftlmalerei.com.

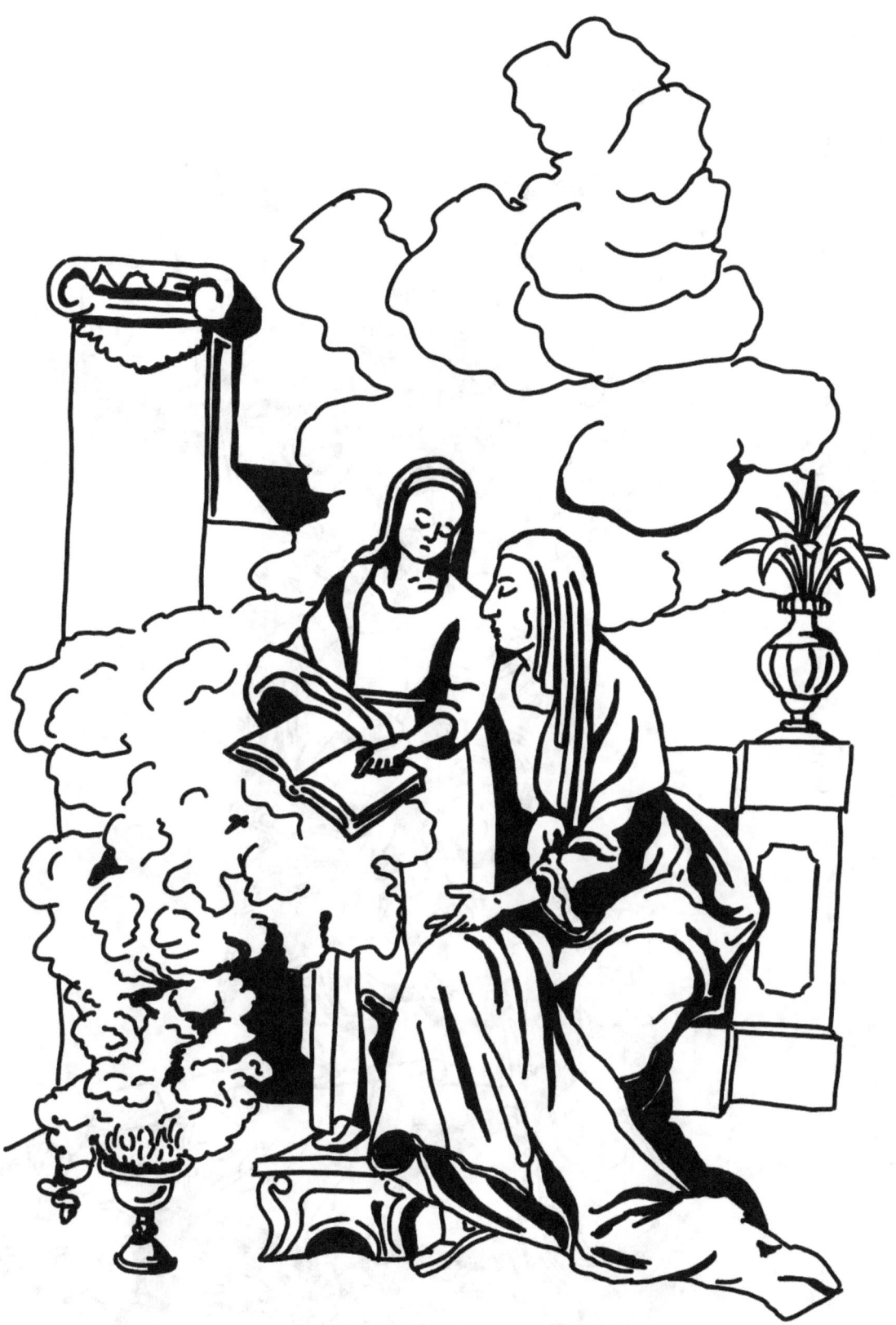

Aumayr's Jewelry Shop, Ludwigstraße 1, painted by Max Kaiser in 1932.

Goldsmith Josef Aumayr first opened his store on Ludwigstrasse in 1919. In 1935, local artist Max Kaiser married Josef's daughter, Anna. Kaiser painted his wife's namesake saint, Saint Anne ("Anna" in German), on the wall above her father's shop. Since the 14th century, artists have depicted Saint Anne, as in the Lüftlmalerei here, teaching her young daughter Mary to read from an open book.

Sieß Bakery, Ludwigstraße 7, painted by Sepp Guggemoos in 1996.

This Lüftlmalerei has the bakers' coat of arms at its center. A pretzel has been the symbol for German bakers since at least the year 1111. Legend has it, during the First Turkish siege of Vienna, in 1529, the Ottoman Turks dug a tunnel under the city wall at night. The bakers, who were awake early and already busy baking, heard the sound of digging, and, when the Turks broke through, fought "like lions." For saving the city, lions ready for battle were added to their coat of arms.

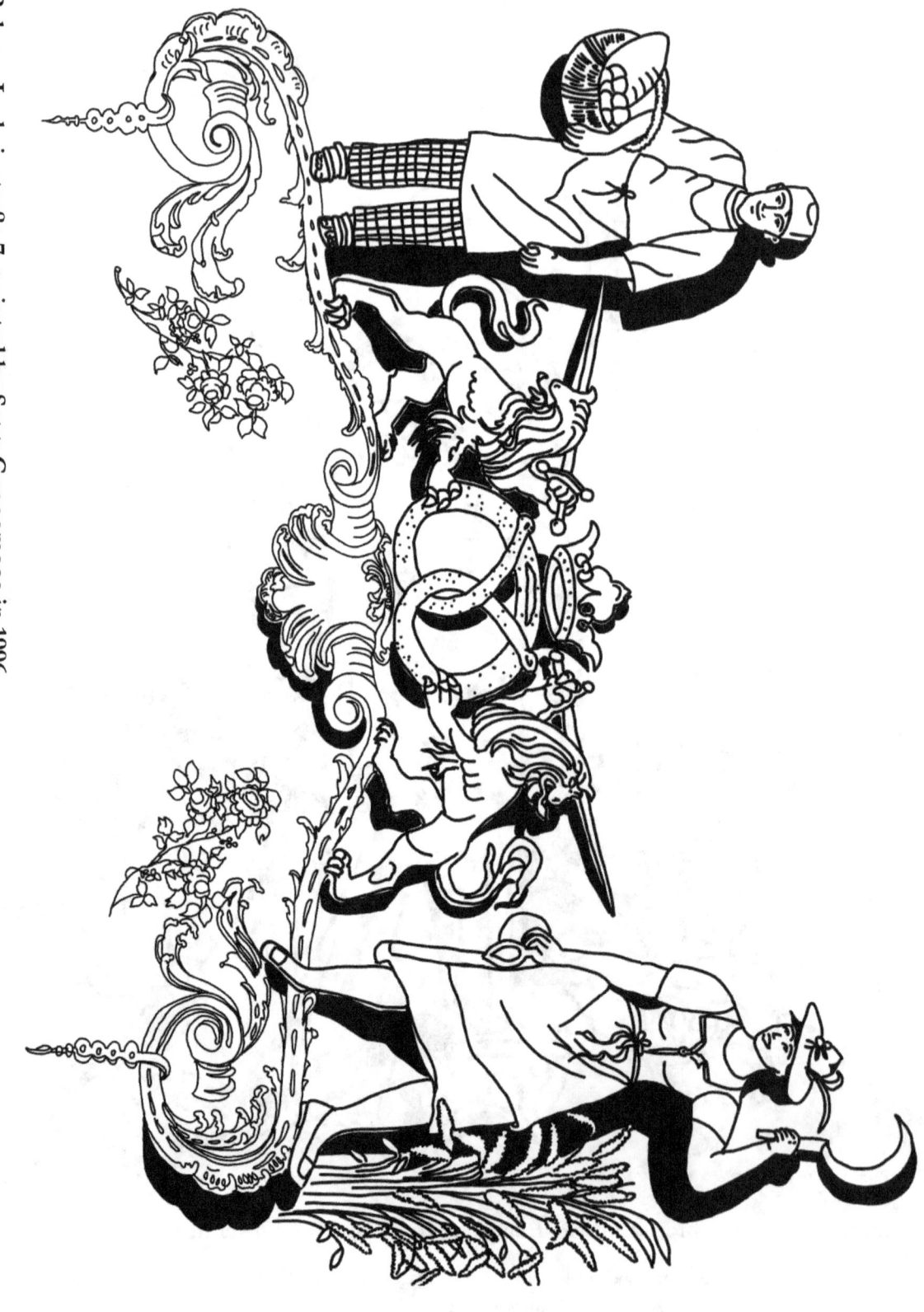

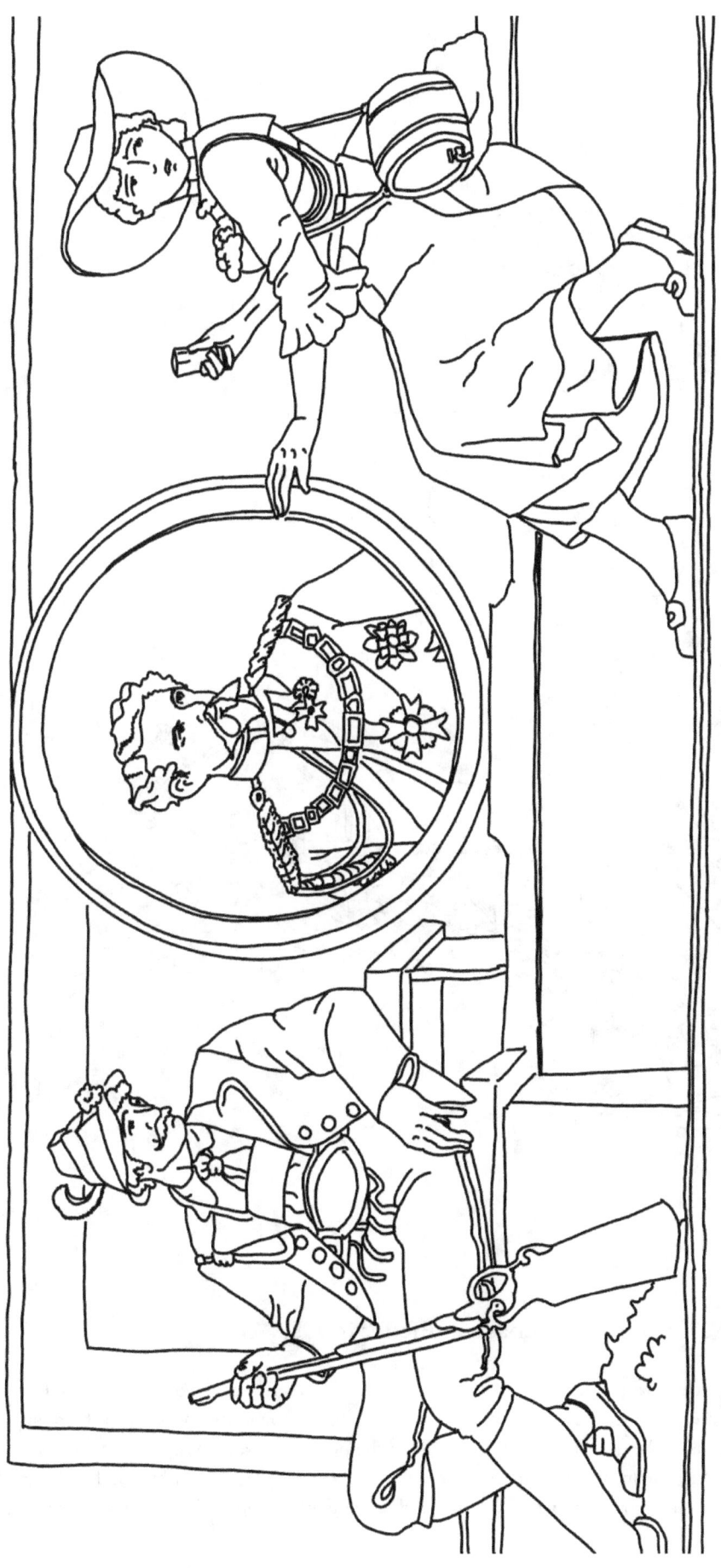

Musik Produktiv, Ludwigstraße 17, painted by Sebastian Pfeffer in 1987.

You can tell by their costumes that he is a sport shooter and the girl is a so-called "sutler." The term dates back to the Middle Ages, when women followed the armies and carried the soldiers' supplies. Even today the term "sutler" is still used in Bavaria for women who accompany a marching or shooting event and supply the musicians or marksmen with drinks.

In between the two is a picture of King Ludwig II of Bavaria (1845 - 1886), the street's namesake. This particular picture of the king is a reproduction of a portrait painted in 1879 by the artist Karl von Piloty.

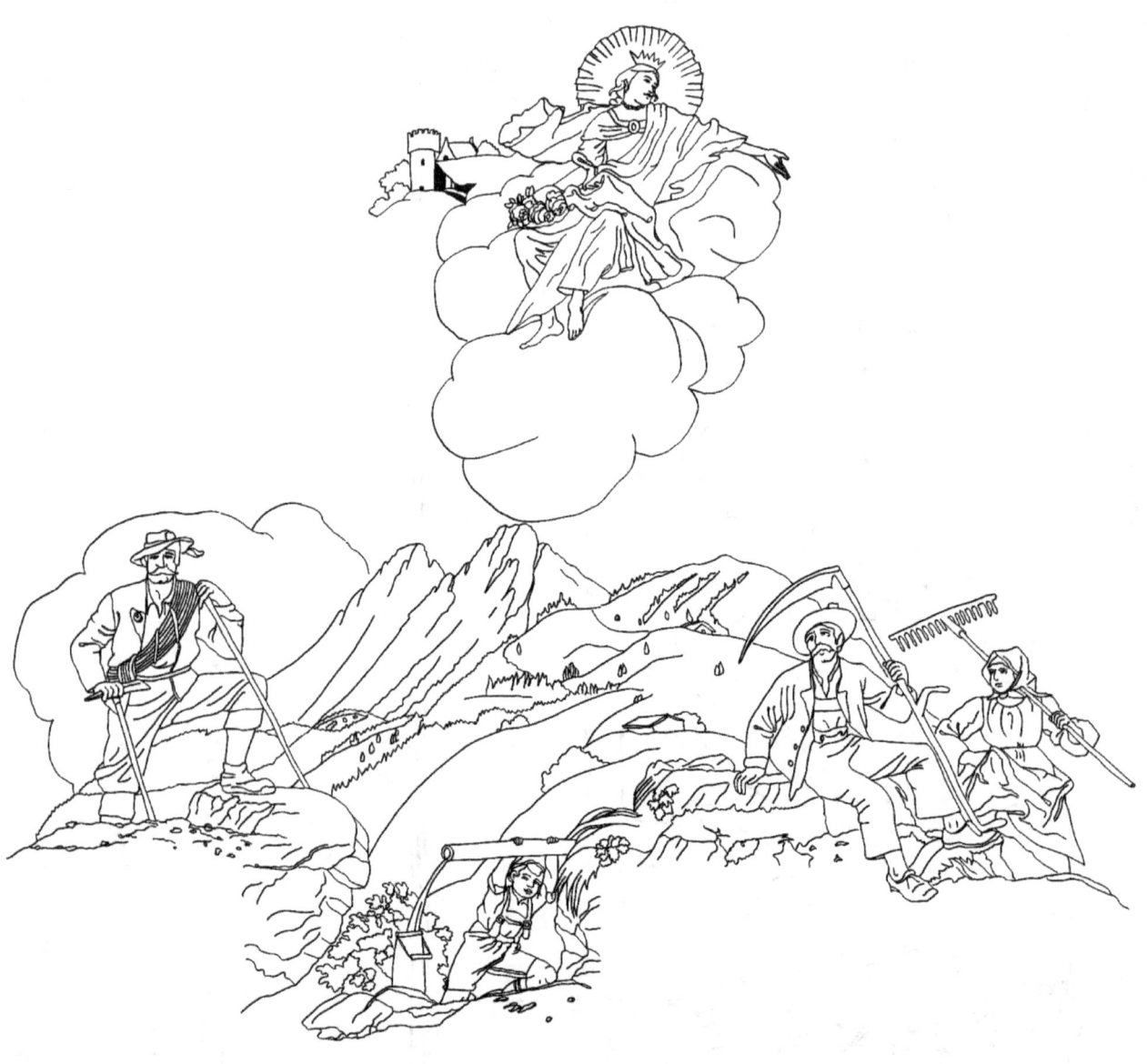

Musik Produktiv, Ludwigstraße 17, painted by Sebastian Pfeffer in 1987.

Floating in the clouds above this Alpine scene is Saint Elizabeth. Born in 1207, Saint Elizabeth was the daughter of the King and Queen of Hungary. As a child, she was taken to live with the family of her future husband in Thuringia, in Germany. There, she was badly treated. In her loneliness, she devoted her time to helping the poor. As legend has it, on one occasion, she left the castle with her apron full of kitchen scraps for the hungry. On her way, she chanced upon her husband. Believing she was stealing from him, he demanded she show him what she was hiding. When she opened her apron, however, miraculously, all he saw were roses.

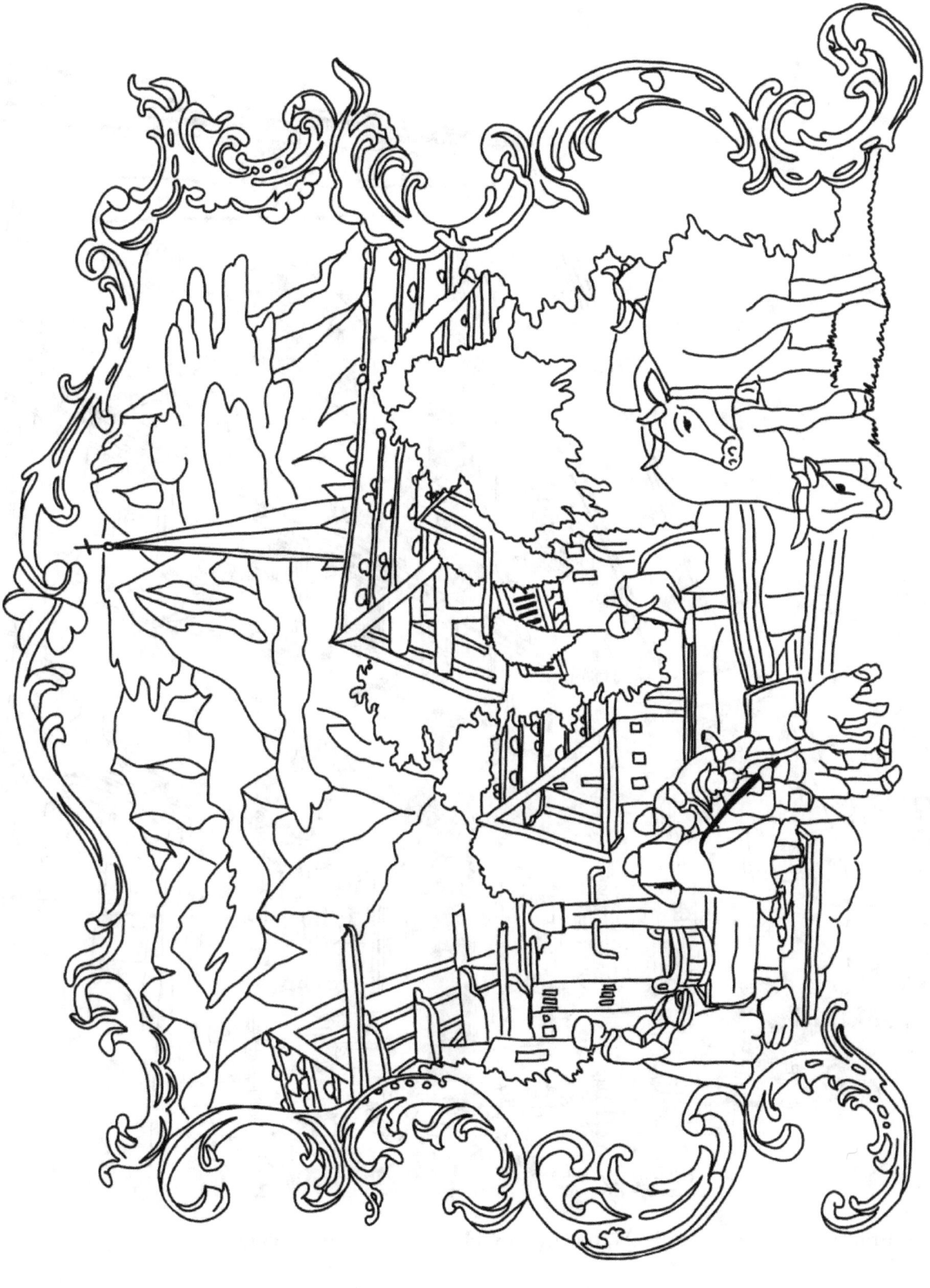

The Schönegger Cheese Alm, Ludwigstraße 22, painted by Sepp Guggemoos in 1985.

An image of women washing laundry in the fountain on Ludwigstrasse in the 19th century, with the Wetterstein mountain range behind them in the skyline.

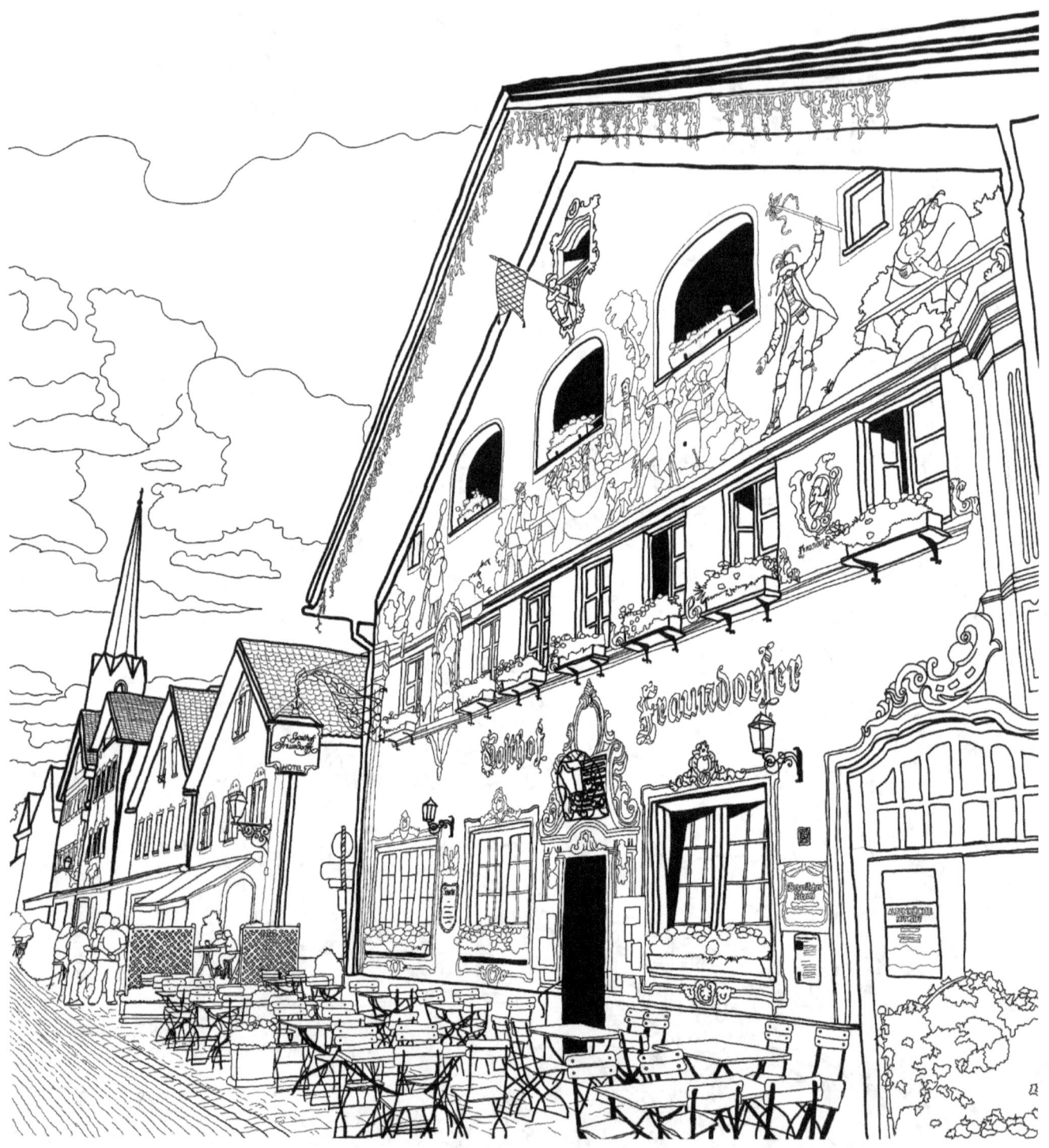

Gasthof Fraundorfer, Ludwigstraße 24, painted by Heinrich Bickel in 1949.

With its traditional Bavarian food, live music, and Schuhplattler dancers, the Gasthof Fraundorfer has been a landmark on this street for almost 100 years. Josef Fraundorfer bought and renovated the building into this restaurant and hotel in 1929. Its front facade with its epic Lüftlmalerei depicts a Bavarian wedding, including the toasting bride and groom, guests, and the traditional master of ceremonies, the "*Hochzeitslader*" – literally, the "Wedding Inviter."

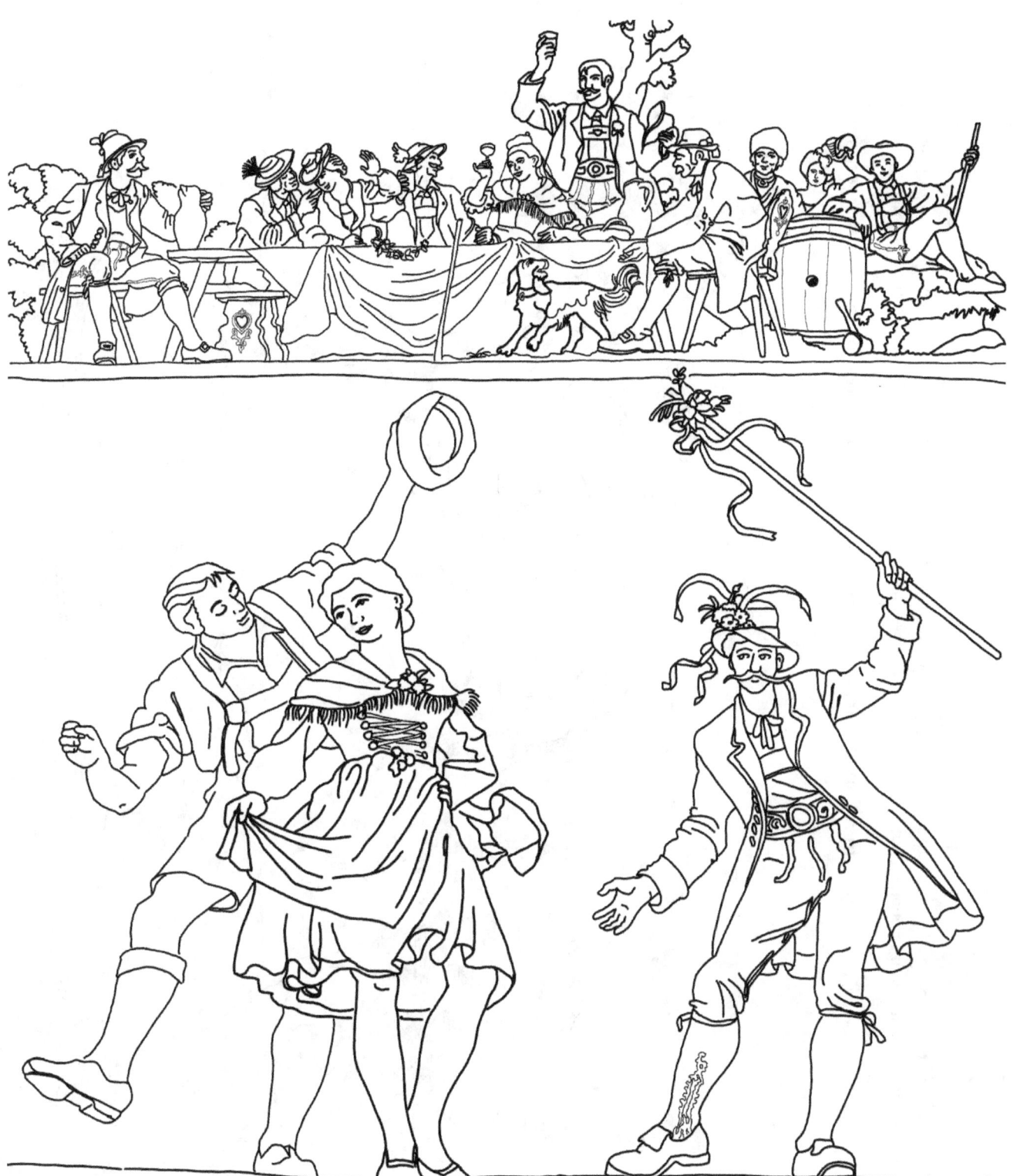

Gasthof Fraundorfer, Ludwigstraße 24, painted by Heinrich Bickel in 1949.

The Hochzeitlader is identified by the carved wooden stick he carries, the "*Ladstecken*," decorated with different colored ribbons in red (symbolizing "love"), blue (symbolizing "loyalty"), green ("hope"), and white ("virginity"). The tradition of the Hochzeitlader dates back to the 16th century, before there was a postal system, when he was the one who went door to door and invited the guests to the wedding. At the wedding itself, Hochzeitlader are a combination of wedding planner and master of ceremonies. He's the one who leads the wedding procession to the church, arranges the seating, organizes the dance and the dinner, sings, dances, teases the bride and groom, makes jokes, and ensures that everyone has a good time.

Former Gasthof Zum Hirschen, Ludwigstraße 32, renovated by Georg Rieger in 1997.

The Lüftlmalerei shows a horse drawn carriage carrying supplies on the road to Partenkirchen with the Wetterstein mountain range in the background. This is another reference to the "*Rottstraße*," the trade route that once passed through here during the "*Rotthandel*," or the time when trade goods came over the passes through the Alps from Italy.

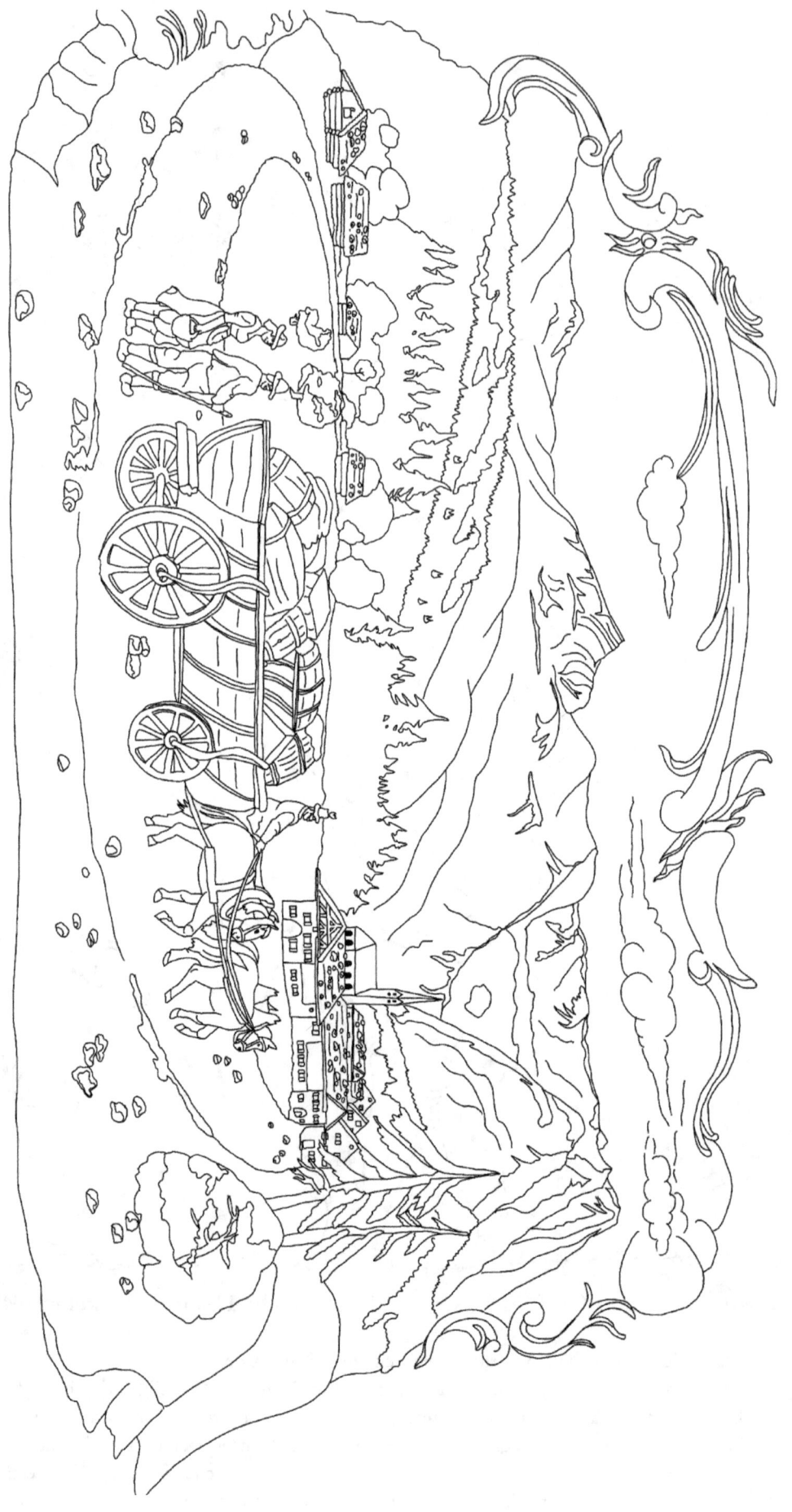

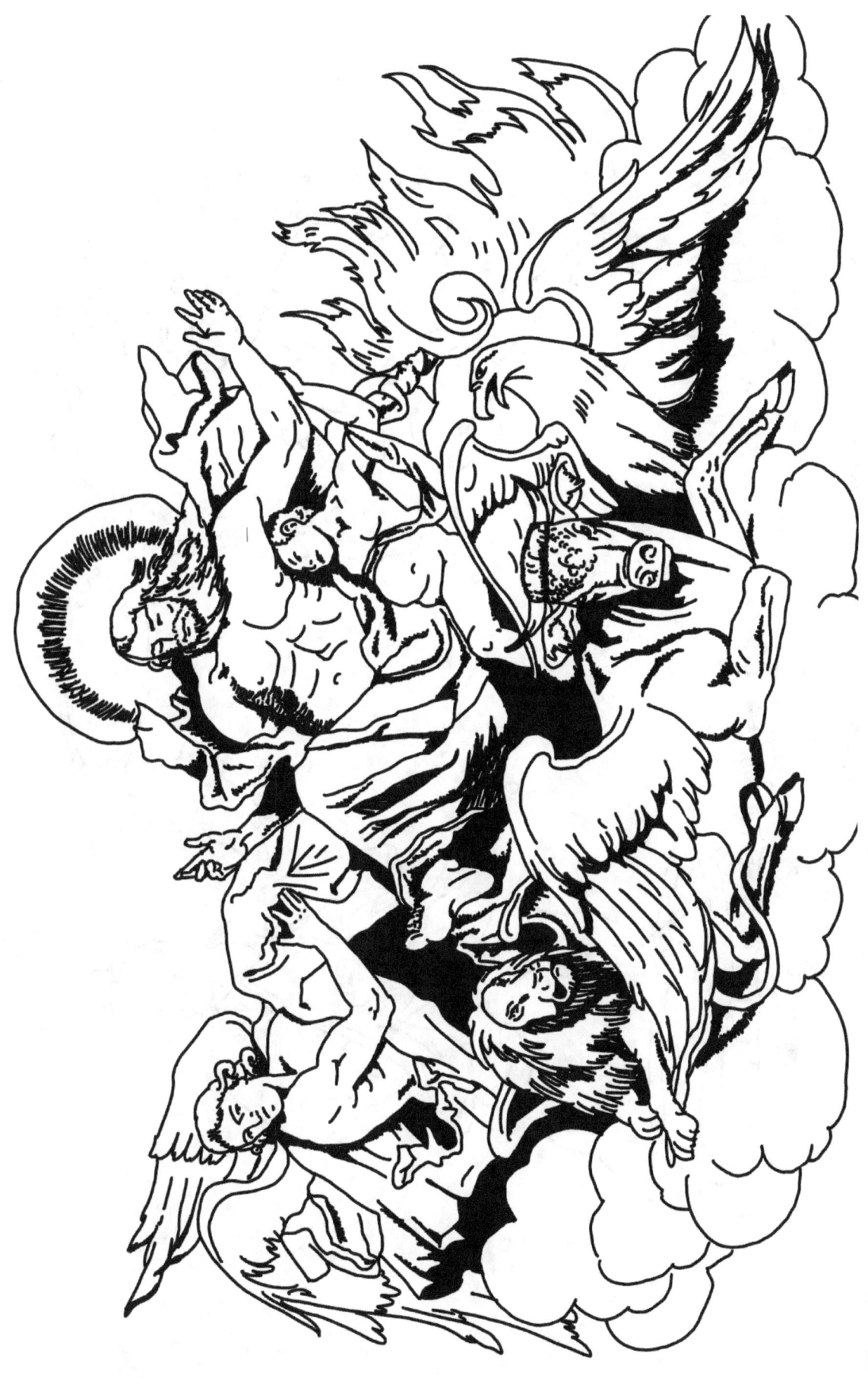

Haus Simon, Ludwigstraße 36, painted by Sebastian Pfeffer in the 1980s.

This particular Lüftlmalerei is a reproduction of The Vision of Ezekiel painted by Raphael in 1518. In the center at the top, God sits on a throne beside Renaissance representations of the four Evangelists, authors of the four Gospels of the New Testament of the Bible: Matthew, a winged man; Mark, a winged lion; Luke, a winged ox; and John, an eagle. These symbols come from the creatures envisioned in the Book of Ezekiel and in the Book of Revelation (Ezekiel 1:3-10 and Revelation 4:6-7).

The former Gasthof zum Melber, Ludwigstraße 37, painted around 1935.

This is a Lüftlmalerei of dancing *Schäfflern* — "coopers," or "barrel makers." In the 1500s, because of the sheer number of breweries in Munich, one of the most prominent trade guilds in the city were the barrel makers. Legend has it, that in 1517, after an outbreak of the plague, when people were still hiding and locked down in their homes, it was the Schäffler guild who first took to the streets and danced. At the sound of their music, the windows opened, and at the sight of their dancing, the frightened people finally dared to leave their homes. In gratitude for the happy end of the plague, the Schäfflern vowed to continue to perform their dance every seven years.

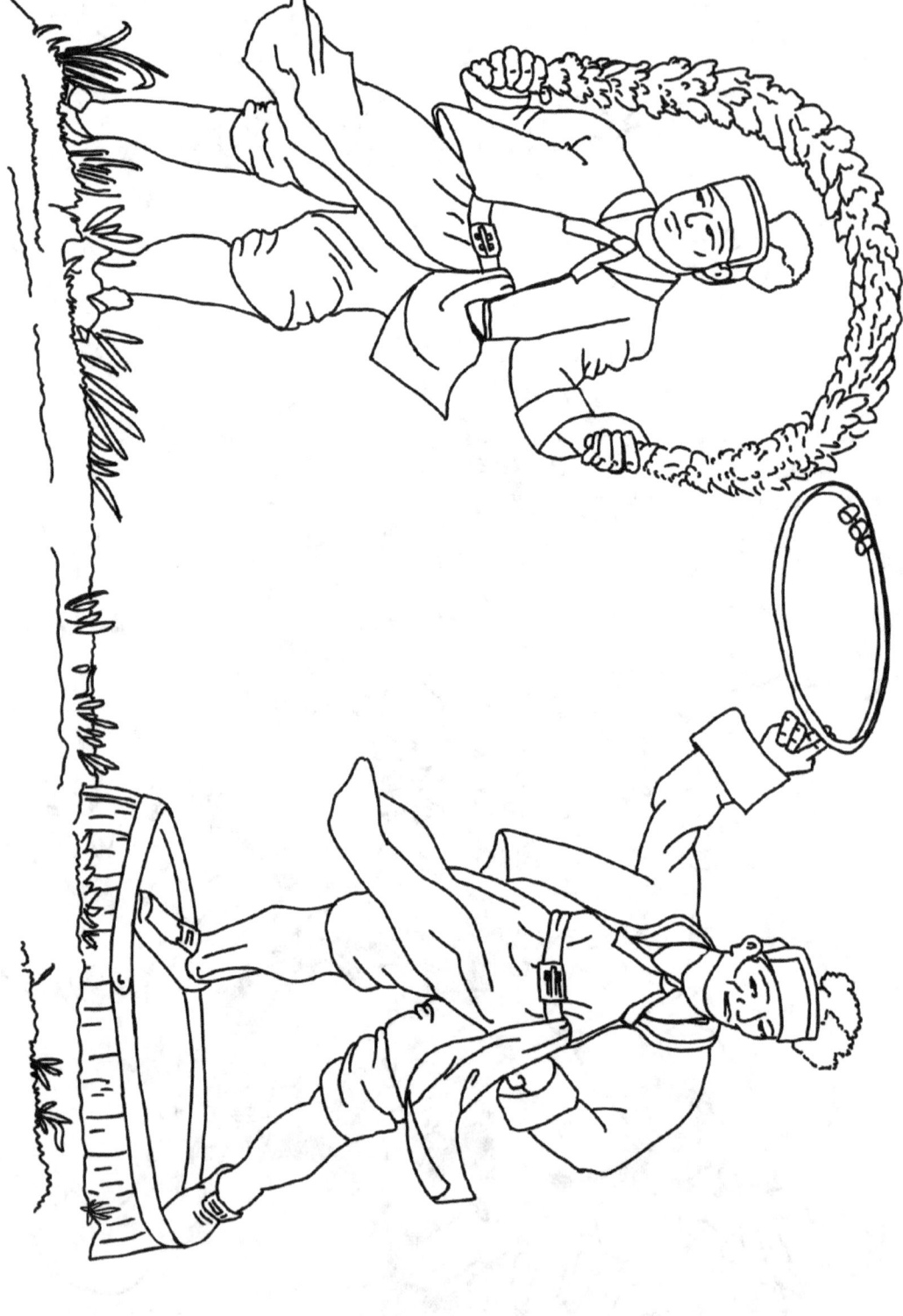

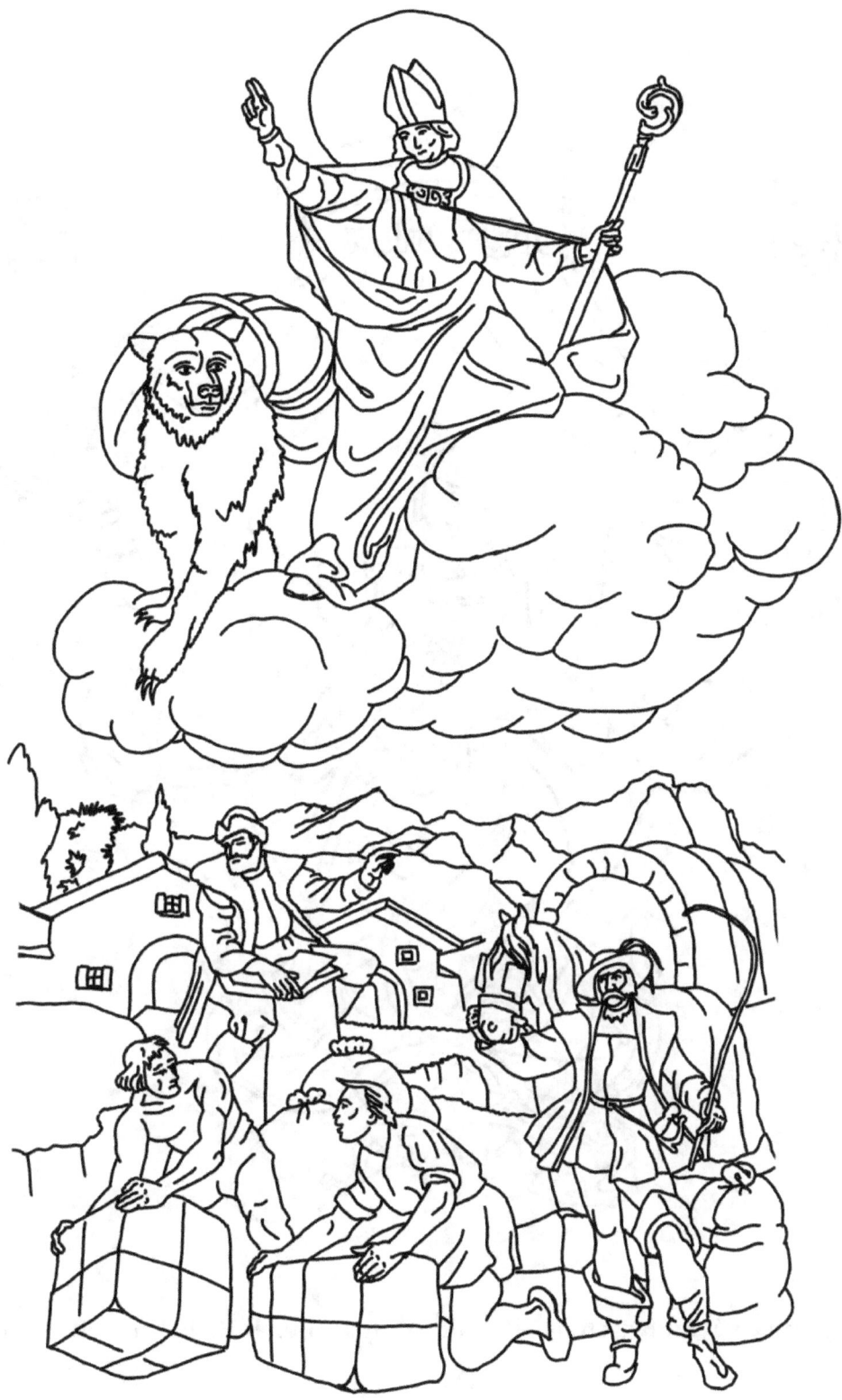

Ludwigstraße 38, painted by Heinrich Bickel around 1950.

A mural of Saint Korbinian in the clouds beside his iconic bear, blessing the merchants and porters below. Legend has it that, while sleeping one night on his way to Rome, a bear crept out of the woods and attacked Korbinian's pack horse. Korbinian awoke to find the bear still gnawing on his horse's carcass, with his pack strewn across the ground. The saint then commanded the bear to carry his load in his horse's place. Once they arrived in Rome, he let the bear go, and it lumbered back to its native forest. Given the legend, Korbinian became the patron saint of porters and carters

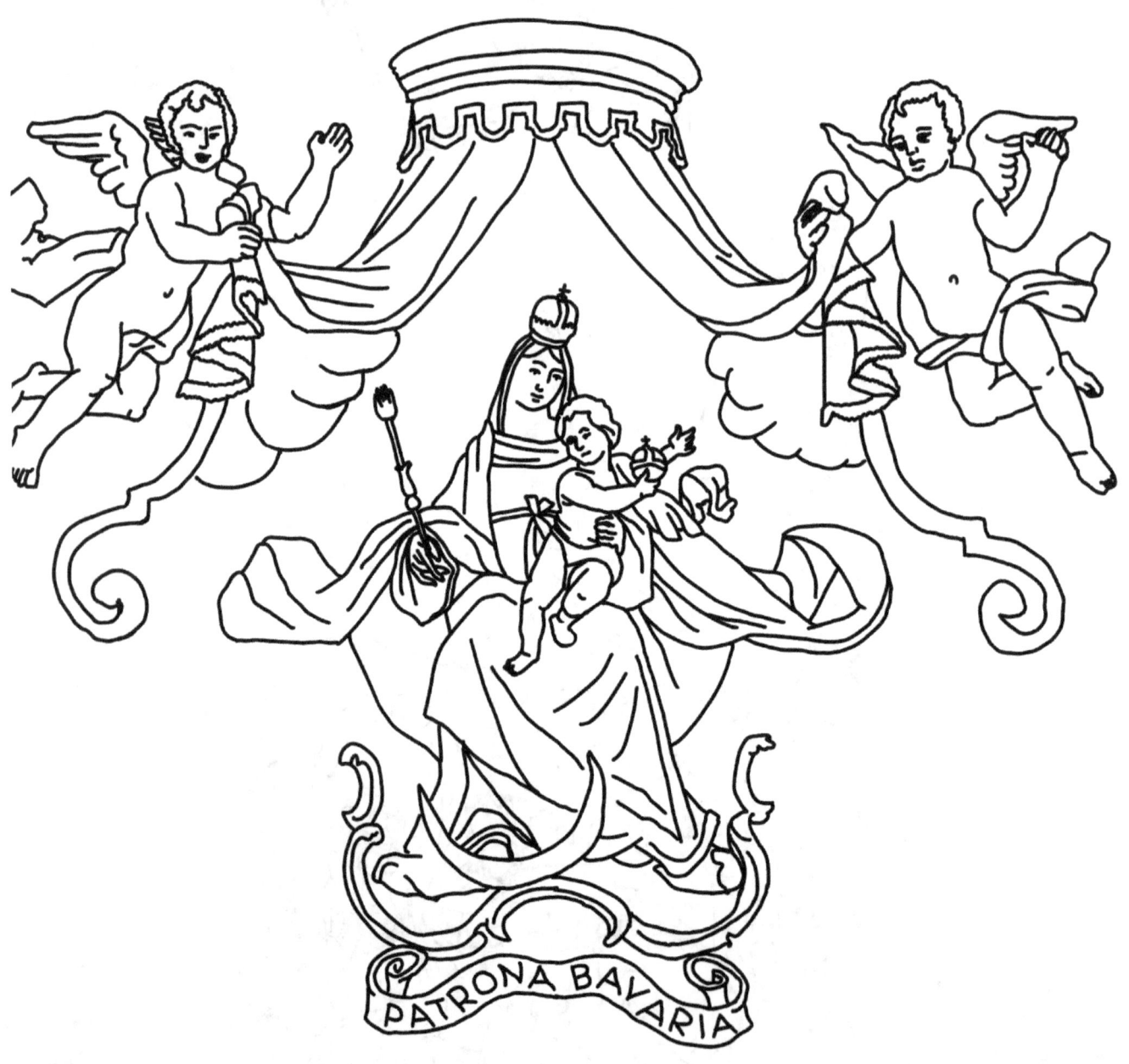

Former bakery and café, Ludwigstraße 41, painted by Heinrich Bickel some time between 1935 and 1945.

Mary as the patron saint of Bavaria (or "*Patrona Bavariae*" in Latin) was first established by Maximilian I (1573-1651) while Duke of Bavaria. In 1616, he had a bronze statue made labeled the "Patrona Boiariae." In the statue, Mary stands with her foot on the crescent moon, with a scepter in her one hand and holding Christ in the other, who, himself holds a globus cruciger (or a cross-topped orb) as a sign of his sovereignty over everything. The statue was fashioned after the vision in the Revelation of John of "a woman clothed with the sun, with the moon under her feet and a crown of twelve stars on her head." (Rev 12:1). However, there are no stars in the Lüftlmalerei here.

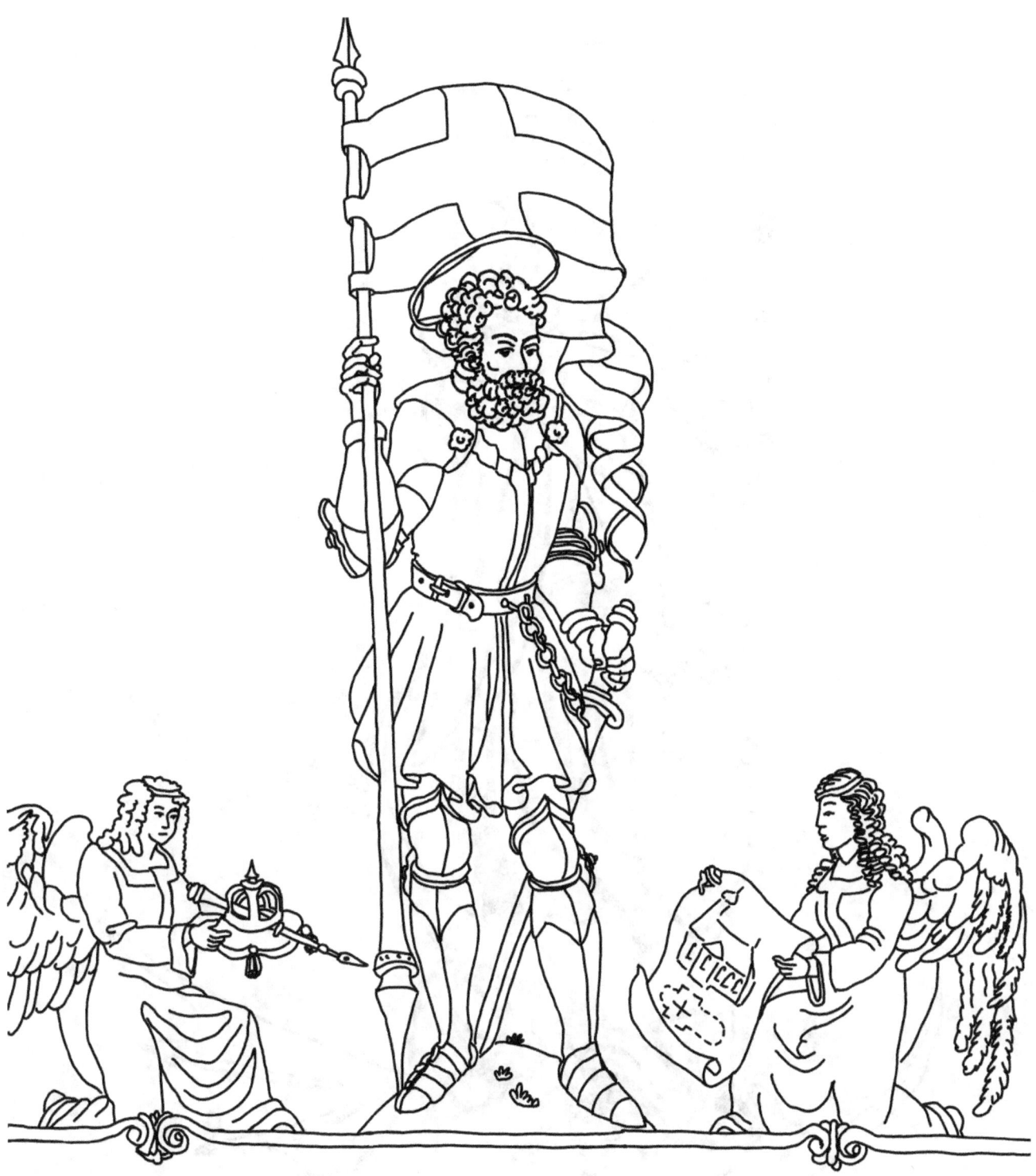

Gasthof zum Rassen, Ludwigstraße 45, renovated by Gerhard Ester in 1988.

The Gasthof zum Rassen is named for Rath of Andechs, a Bavarian count ("*Graf*" in German) military leader, pilgrim, and eventual saint. He led the Bavarians against invading Maegyars (modern day Hungarians) in the tenth century but, legend has it, gave up his title to become a monk. By 1132, so many pilgrims came to worship at the monastery he built where he was buried in the town of Wörth, that the town renamed itself "Grafrath" after him. His bones were later transferred to the town of Diessen and in 1640 a chronicler of his life nicknamed him "Rasso." While he is nearly unheard of today, his cult was once so large that some 12,000 miracles were attributed to his relics between the years 1444 and 1728. Given their value, his bones have been stolen more than once. And they are large bones – Saint Rasso stood over 2 meters (6 ½ feet) tall.

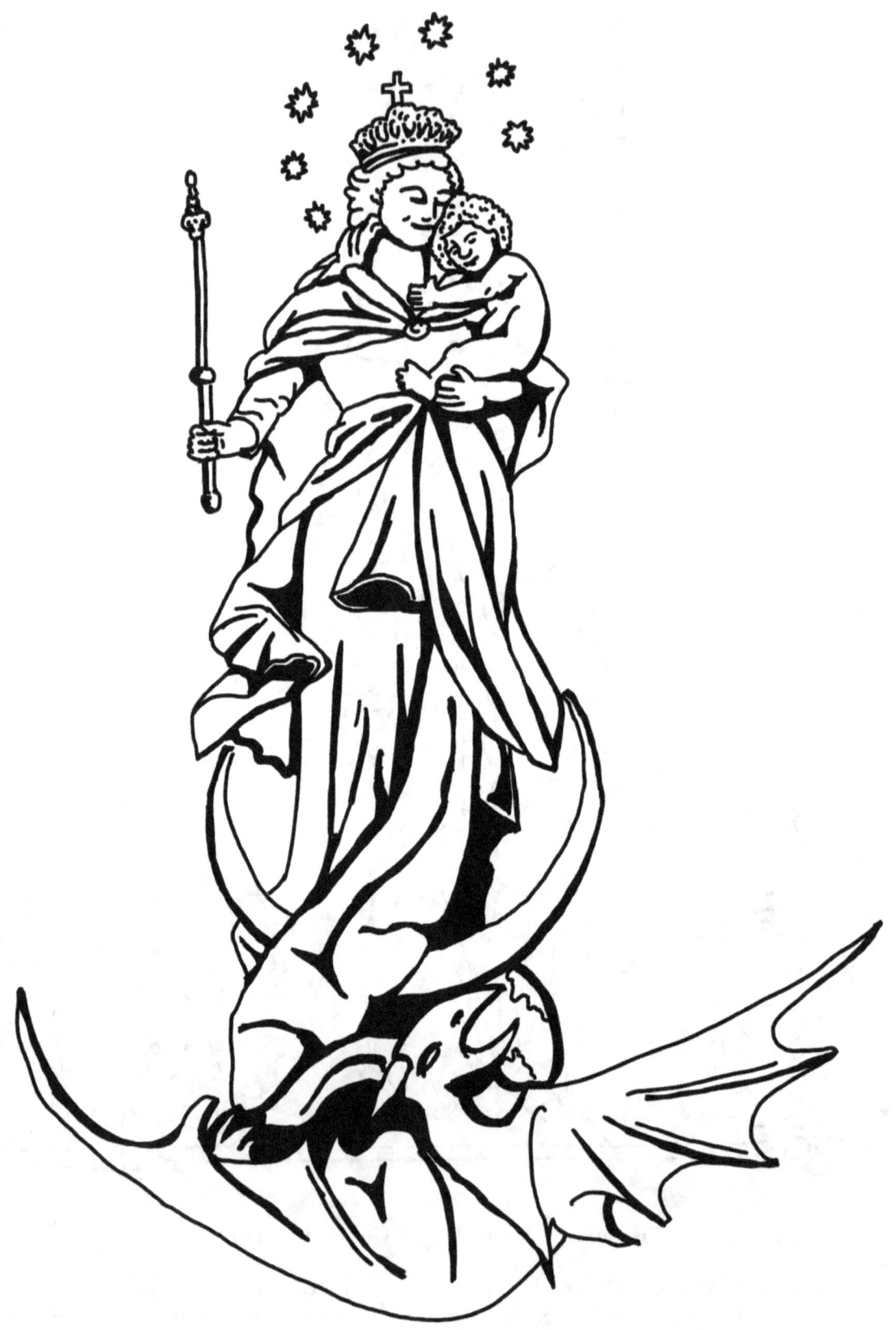

Assumption of the Blessed Virgin Mary Parish Church, Ludwigstraße 46.

During the Thirty Years' War, Maximillian I vowed to build a "godly work" if the city of Munich was spared. In 1638, once he was certain the city was safe, he erected the *Mariensäule*, the "Column of Mary," in Munich's town square. The Latin inscription on the base of the pillar refers to his vow and to Mary for the first time as the patron saint of Bavaria.

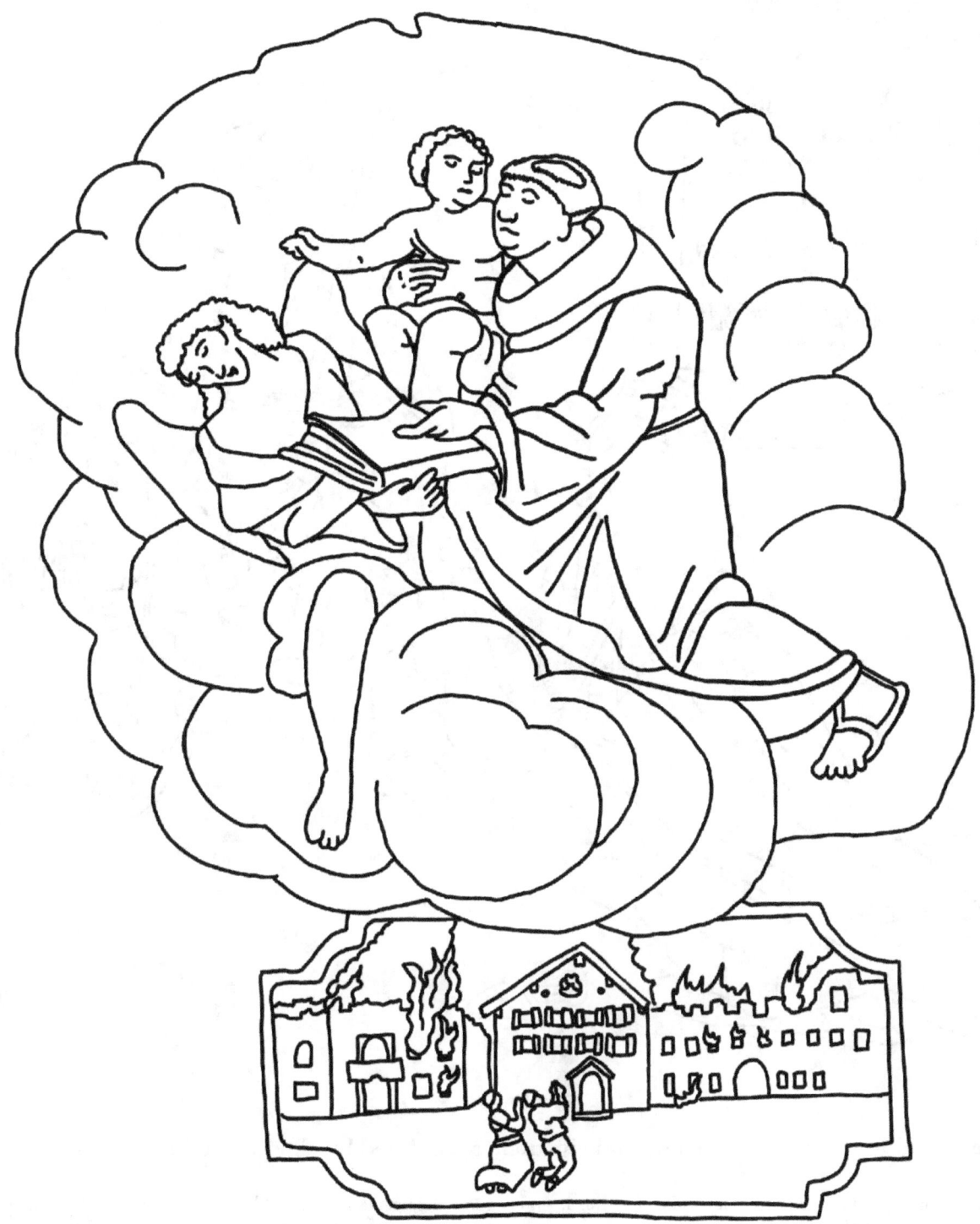

The Werdenfels Museum, Ludwigstraße 47, originally painted around 1747, renovated after 1865.

This building dates back to the 15th century. Since 1973, it has been home to the Werdenfels Museum. It was one of only two buildings on this street to survive the Great Market Fire in 1865. Legend has it that on the day of the fire, a strange woman had asked residents of Ludwigstrasse to let her warm up some milk for her small child. The residents of house number 47 are said to have been the only ones who helped her. Maybe it was this good deed that protected the house from the flames. Or perhaps it was thanks to the protection of Saint Anthony of Padua, as in the Lüftlmalerei painted here.

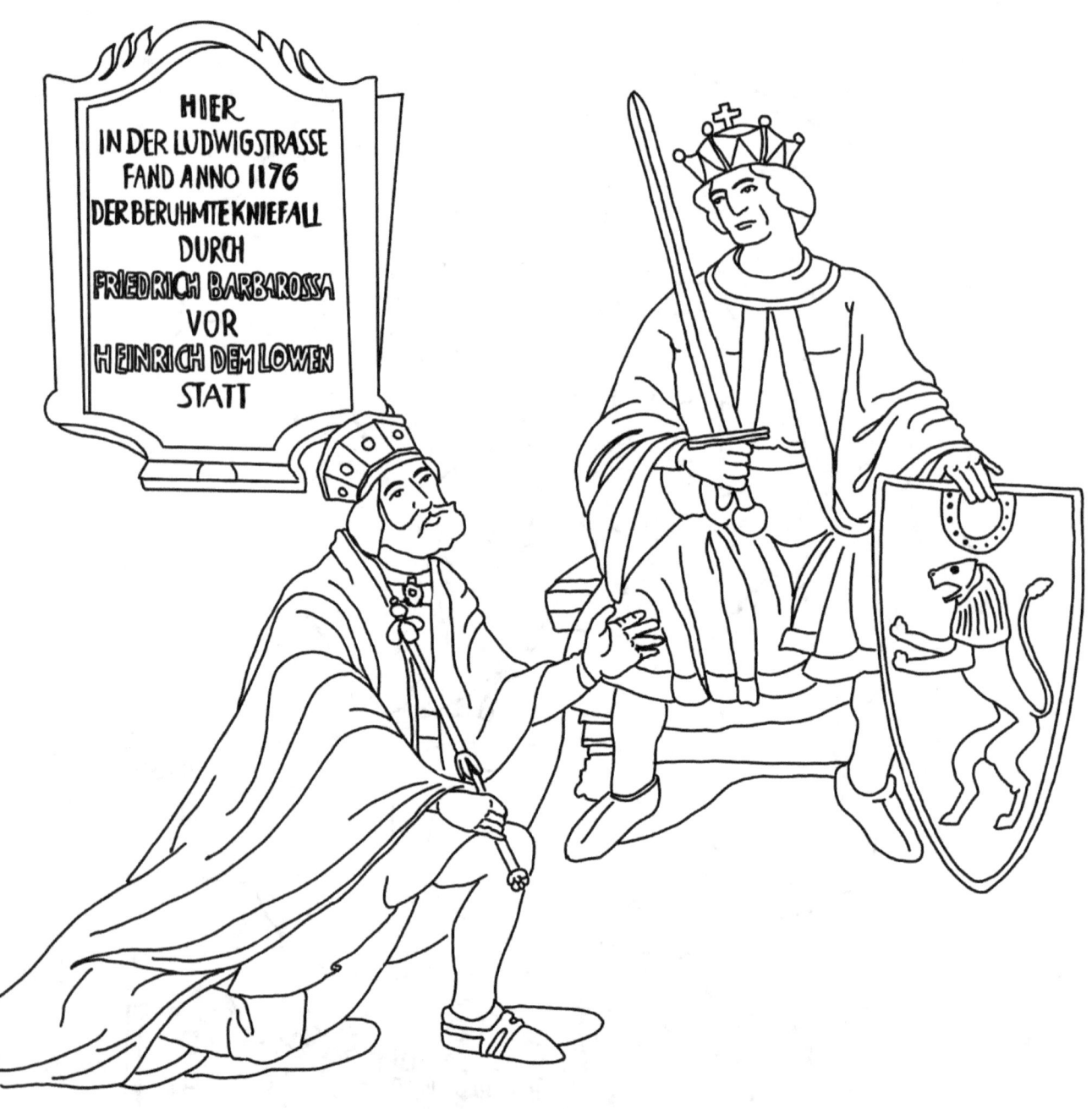

Former Konditorei and Café Liefert, Ludwigstraße 55, painted by Eberhard Hülsmann in 1974.

As the inscription beside the Lüftlmalerei explains, this is an image depicting the moment, "here on Ludwigstraße in the year 1176" when, legend has it, the Holy Roman Emperor Friedrich Barbarossa — "*Barbarossa*" meaning "Red Beard" in Italian — knelt down before Heinrich the Lion, Duke of Bavaria, pleading him for military and financial aid. The Holy Roman Emperor was also king of the Germans and could order the Dukes to do what he wanted. When he begged the Duke of Bavaria to help him wage war against cities in Italy, the Duke of Bavaria refused, saying he only had to obey the Emperor inside the German borders, and therefore would not send soldiers south into Italy. As revenge for the embarrassing moment, in 1180, Emperor Barbarossa declared Heinrich the Lion an outlaw, broke up the Kingdom of Germany into separate fiefs and redrew the borders, giving the family of the House of Wittelsbach control of Bavaria — a dynasty that ruled Bavaria until 1918.

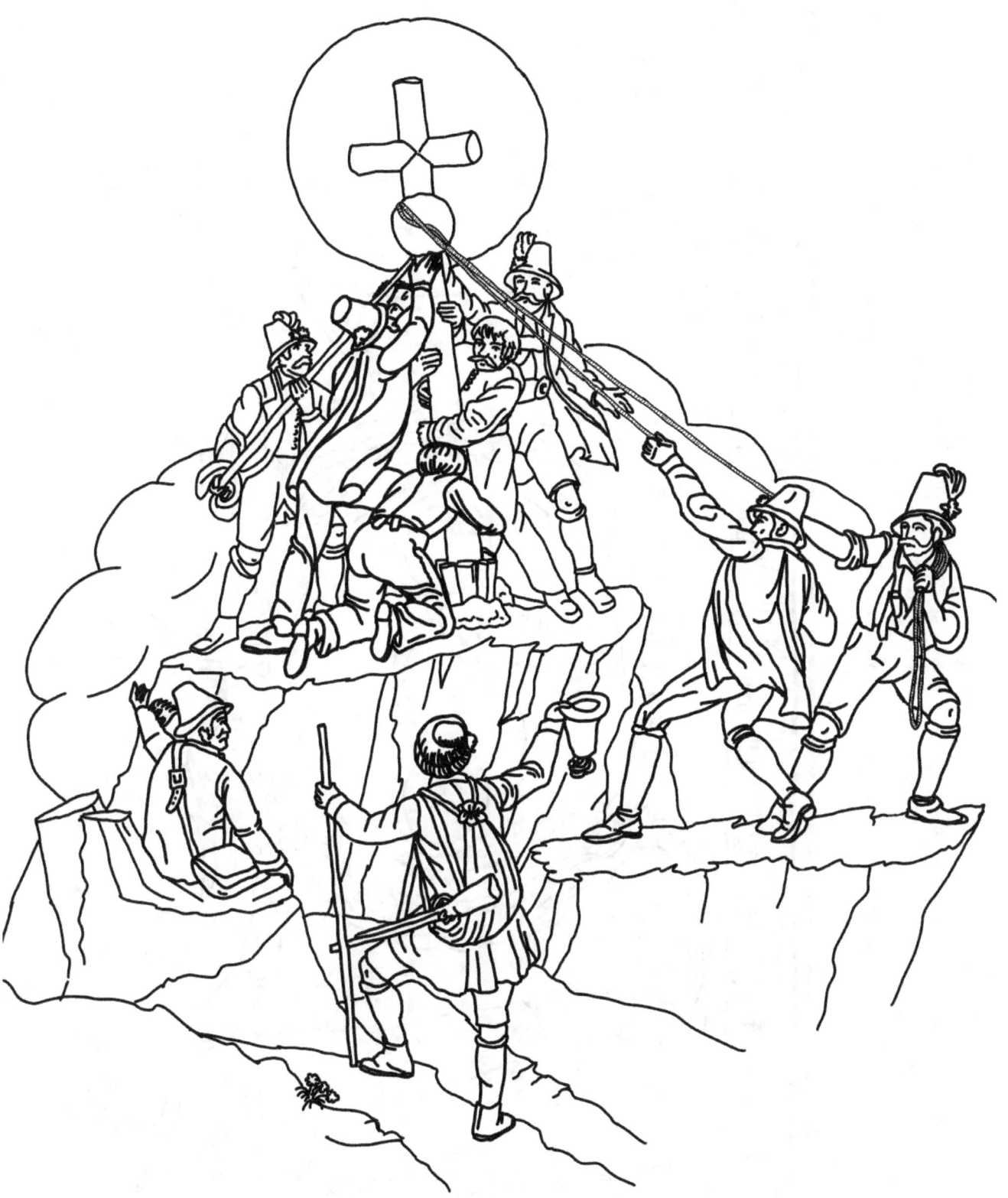

Former Konditorei and Café Liefert, Ludwigstraße 55, painted by Eberhard Hülsmann in 1974.

Just south of Garmisch-Partenkirchen, straddling the border between Germany and Austria, at 2,962 meters (or 9,718 feet) above sea level, the Zugspitze is the tallest mountain in Germany. This Lüftlmalerei depicts the 28 citizens of Partenkirchen who climbed the Zugspitze to put a cross on the top on August 14, 1851.

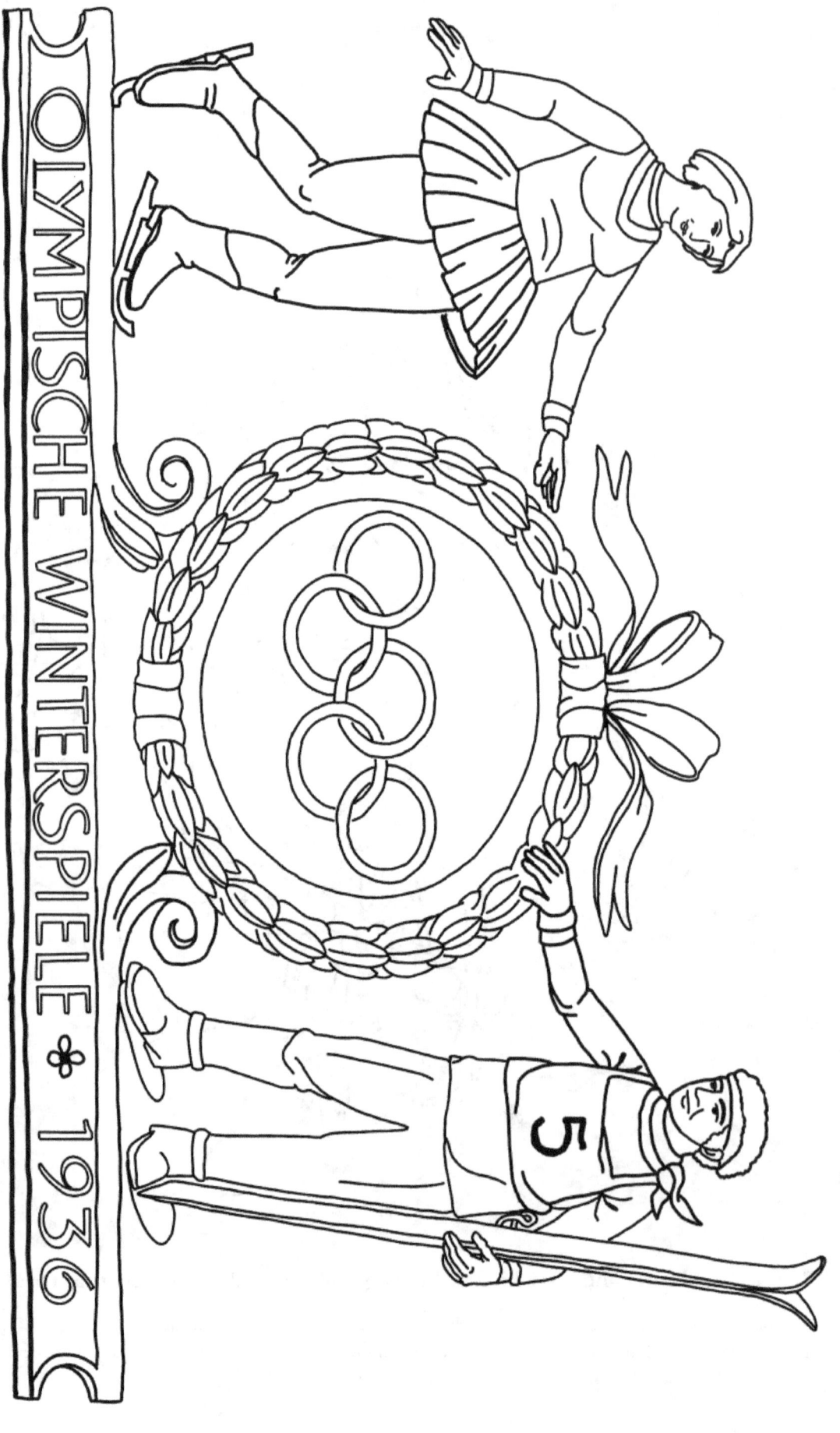

Former Konditorei and Café Liefert, Ludwigstraße 55, painted by Eberhard Hülsmann in 1974. Garmisch and Partenkirchen — two towns separated for centuries by the Partnach River — were combined on January 1, 1935, by order of Adolf Hitler for the Olympic Winter Games. In addition to literally putting the combined town of Garmisch-Partenkirchen on the map, the 1936 Olympic Winter Games marked the beginning of mass tourism and cemented the town's reputation as the winter sports travel destination it is today.

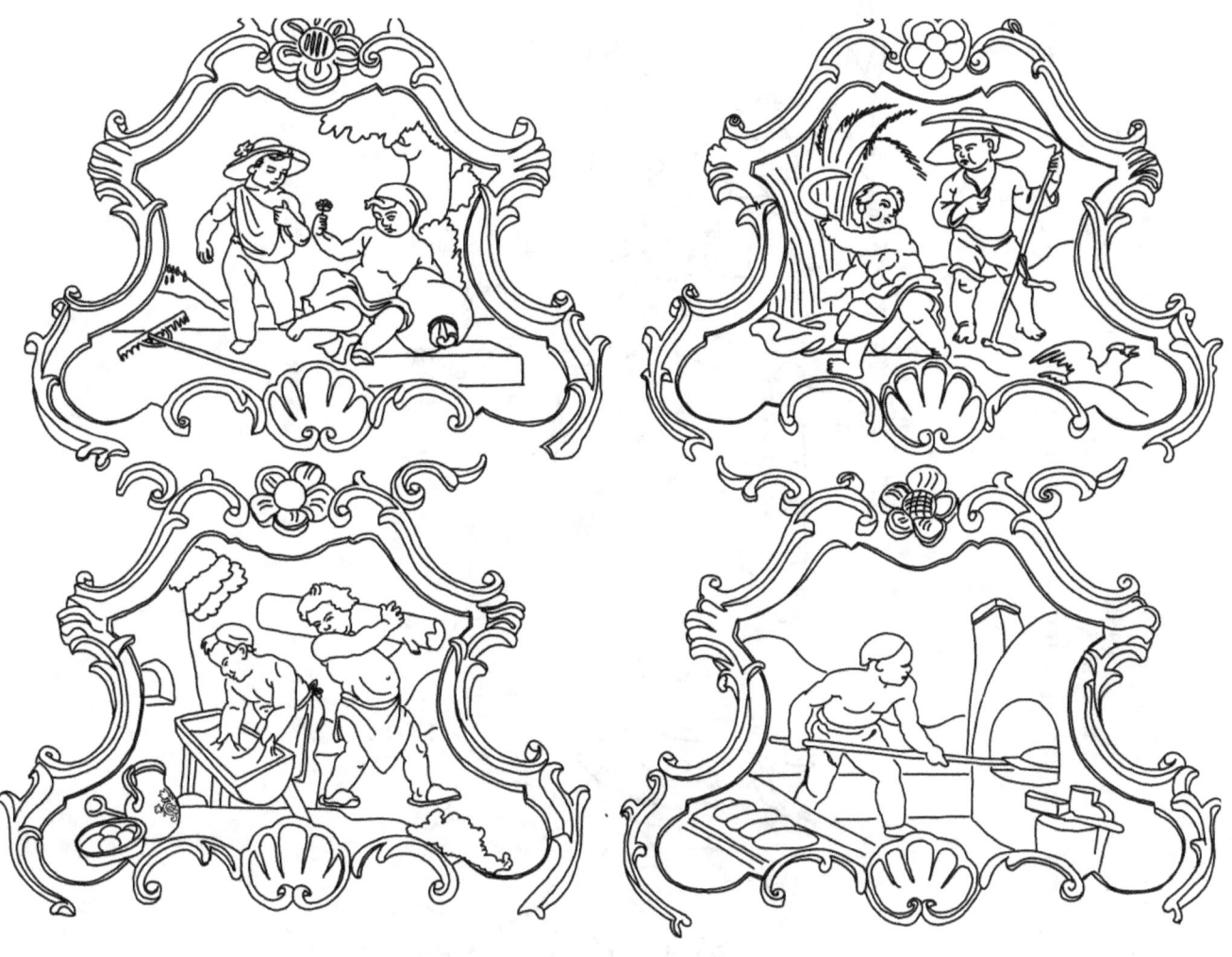

The former bakery zum Langer-Beck, Ludwigstraße 56, painted by Heinrich Bickel some time between 1925 and 1935.

A *putto* is the name for the chubby child figure, often depicted with wings, frequently appearing in both mythological and religious art from the Renaissance – like Cupid, for example. The wingless and rather muscular *putti* here work in all the positions required to bake bread – planting and harvesting wheat, making dough, and baking bread – fitting symbols on the wall of this former bakery.

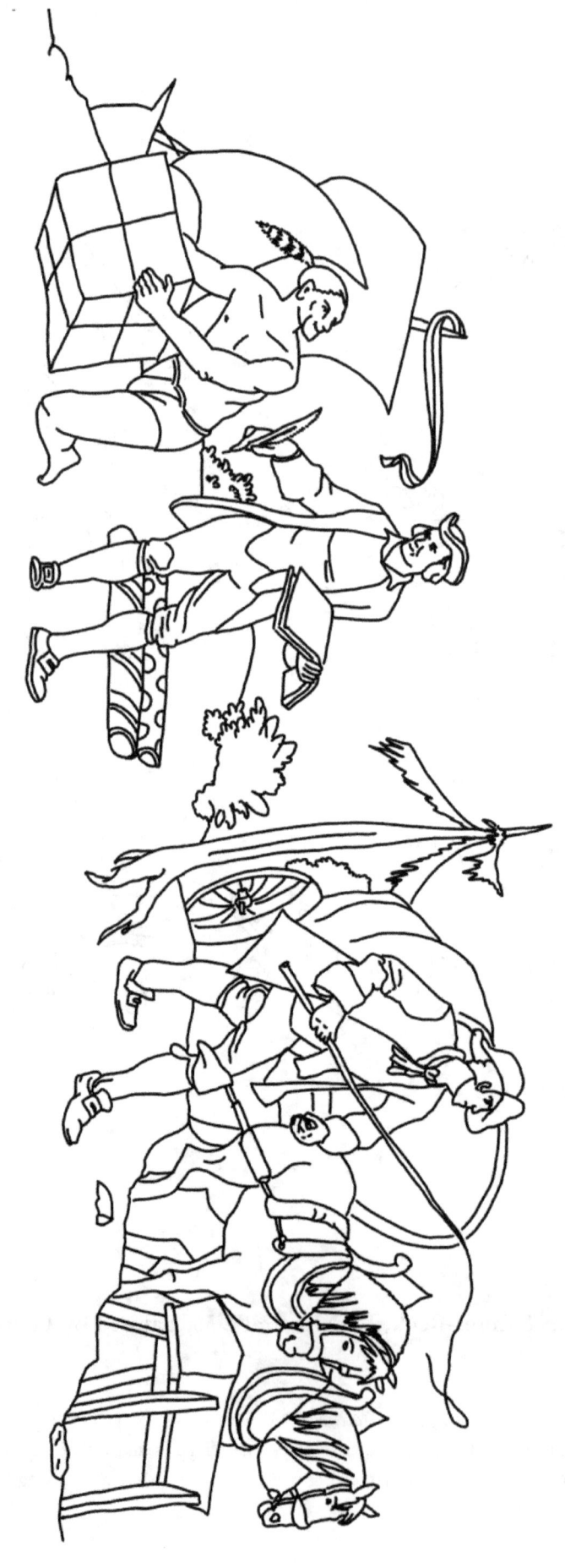

Former Department Store Kögl, Ludwigstraße 61, painted by Heinrich Bickel around 1950.

The discovery of America fundamentally changed the transport routes in Europe. What's more, it fundamentally changed the items traded in Europe, as new fruits, vegetables, and livestock arrived in the Old World. What, after all, would Italian food be without tomato sauce? Or German food be without potatoes? – Both of which were brought back from the Americas.

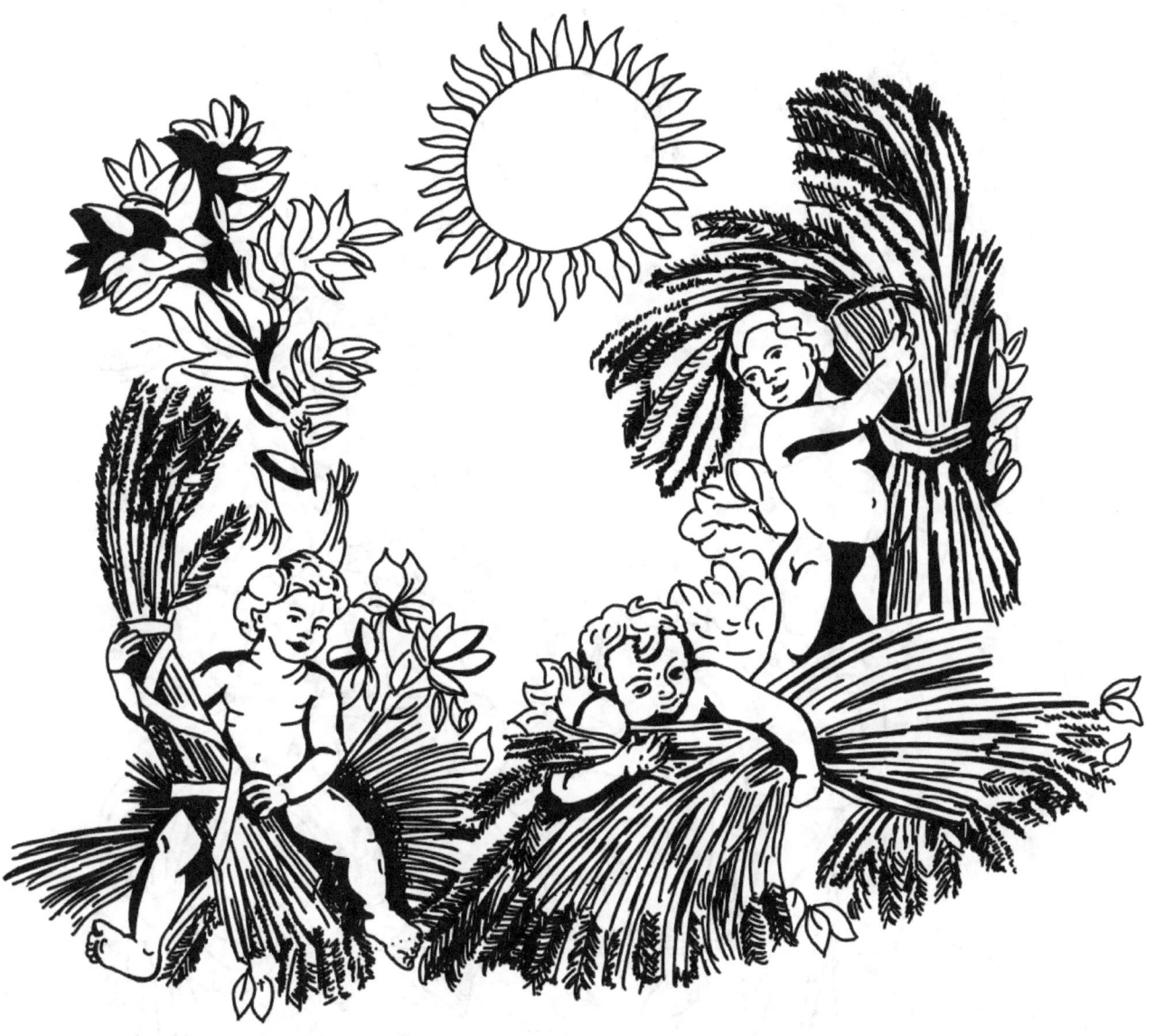

Ludwigstraße 72.

The putti harvesting wheat in the Lüftlmalerei here are a bit of a mystery.

The artist who painted this mural did not sign or date it, and whoever had it painted is (so far) keeping its history a secret.

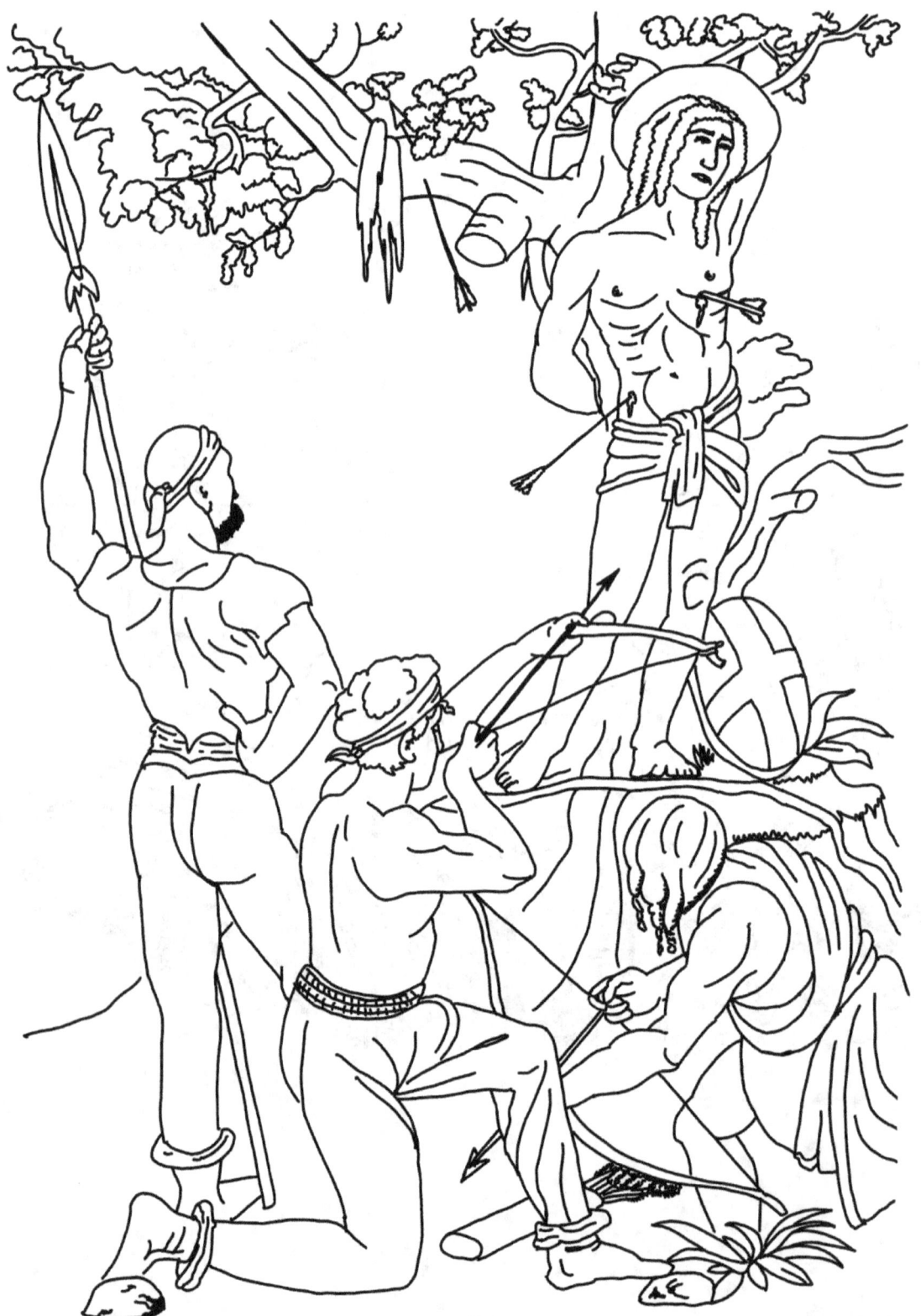

Ludwigstraße 79, by Heinrich Bickel around 1935, most recently renovated by Michele Nardiello.

According to legend, Saint Sebastian was killed during the persecution of Roman Emperor Diocletian. At first, he was tied to a tree and shot with arrows. However, when this did not kill him, he was eventually clubbed to death, instead. Saint Sebastian became a popular subject in 17th century paintings, as boils or sores commonly associated with the plague reminded people of arrow wounds. Fittingly, this Lüftlmalerei is painted on the building facing the Saint Sebastian Chapel directly across the street.

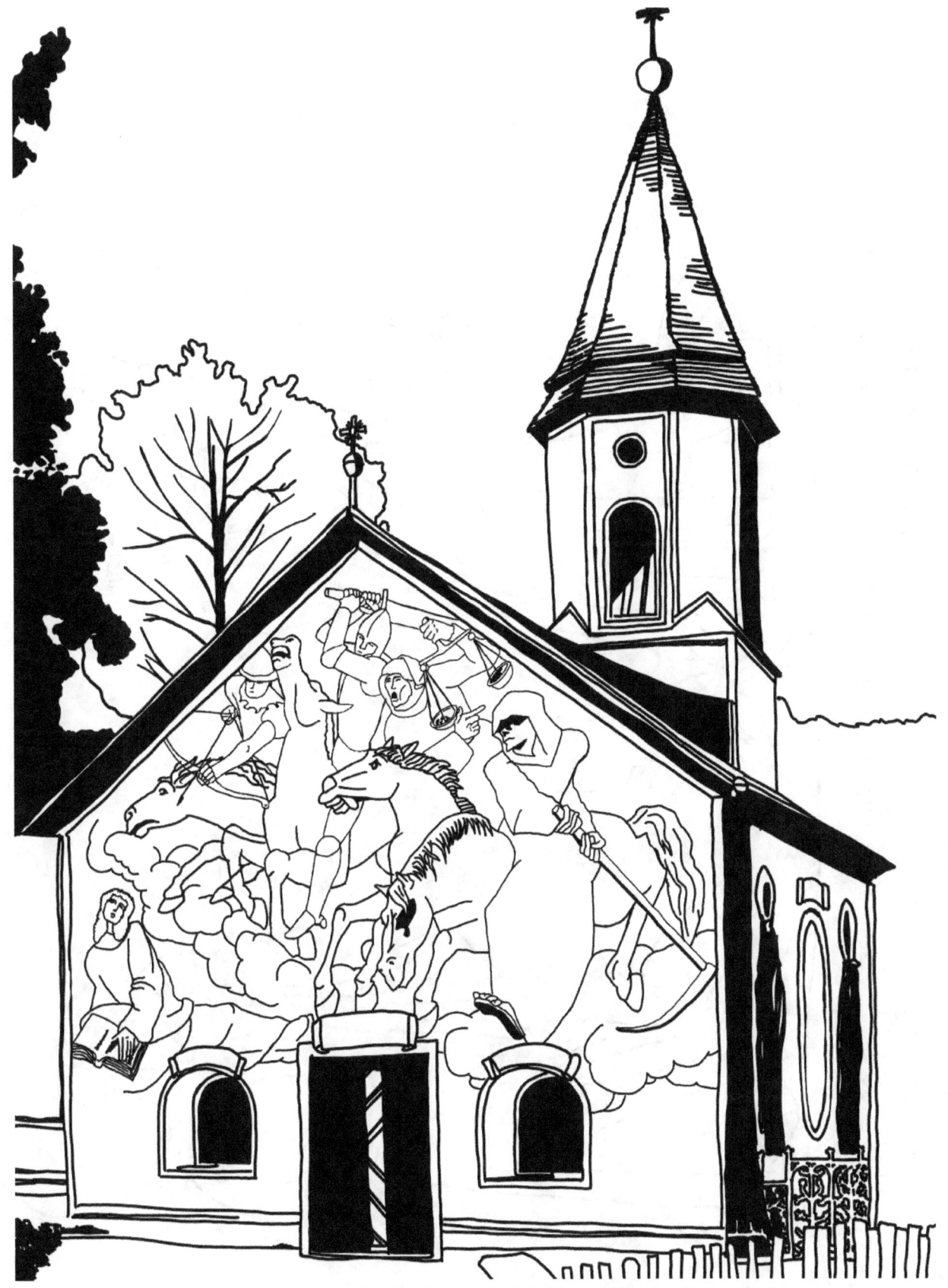

Saint Sebastian Chapel, Münchner Straße 1, painted by Josef Wackerle in 1924.

First consecrated in 1673 to Saints Sebastian and Rochus, the patron saints against the plague, this was once the site of the cemetery for plague victims. Renovated in 1924, the cemetery was replaced with a memorial to soldiers lost in World War I. On the outside wall of the chapel, a Lüftlmalerei of John and his revelation of the Four Horsemen of the Apocalypse: "Pestilence" (another word for "plague") shooting arrows, "War" with a sword, "Famine" carrying scales, and "Death" wielding a scythe.

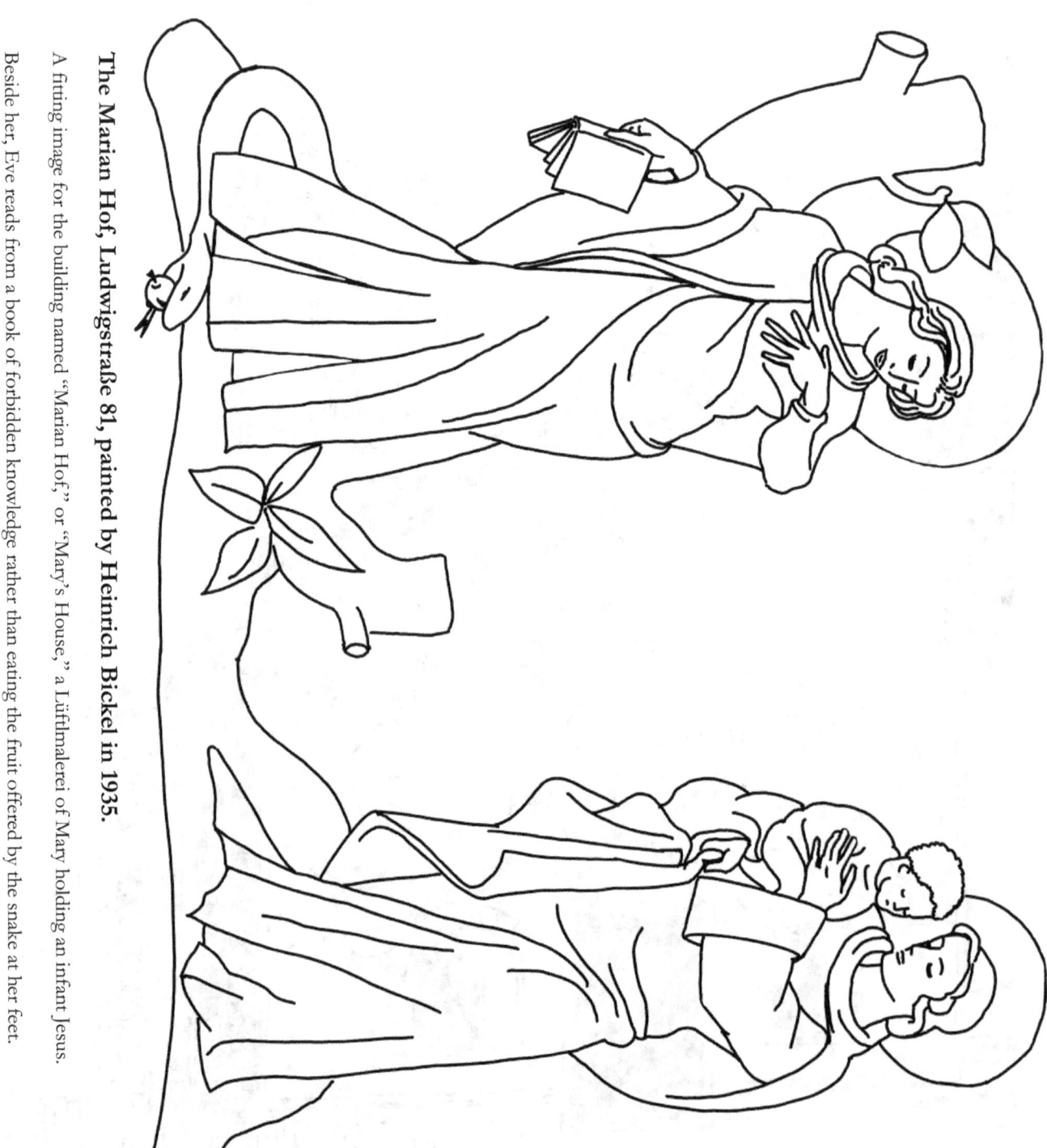

The Marian Hof, Ludwigstraße 81, painted by Heinrich Bickel in 1935.

A fitting image for the building named "Marian Hof," or "Mary's House," a Lüftlmalerei of Mary holding an infant Jesus. Beside her, Eve reads from a book of forbidden knowledge rather than eating the fruit offered by the snake at her feet.

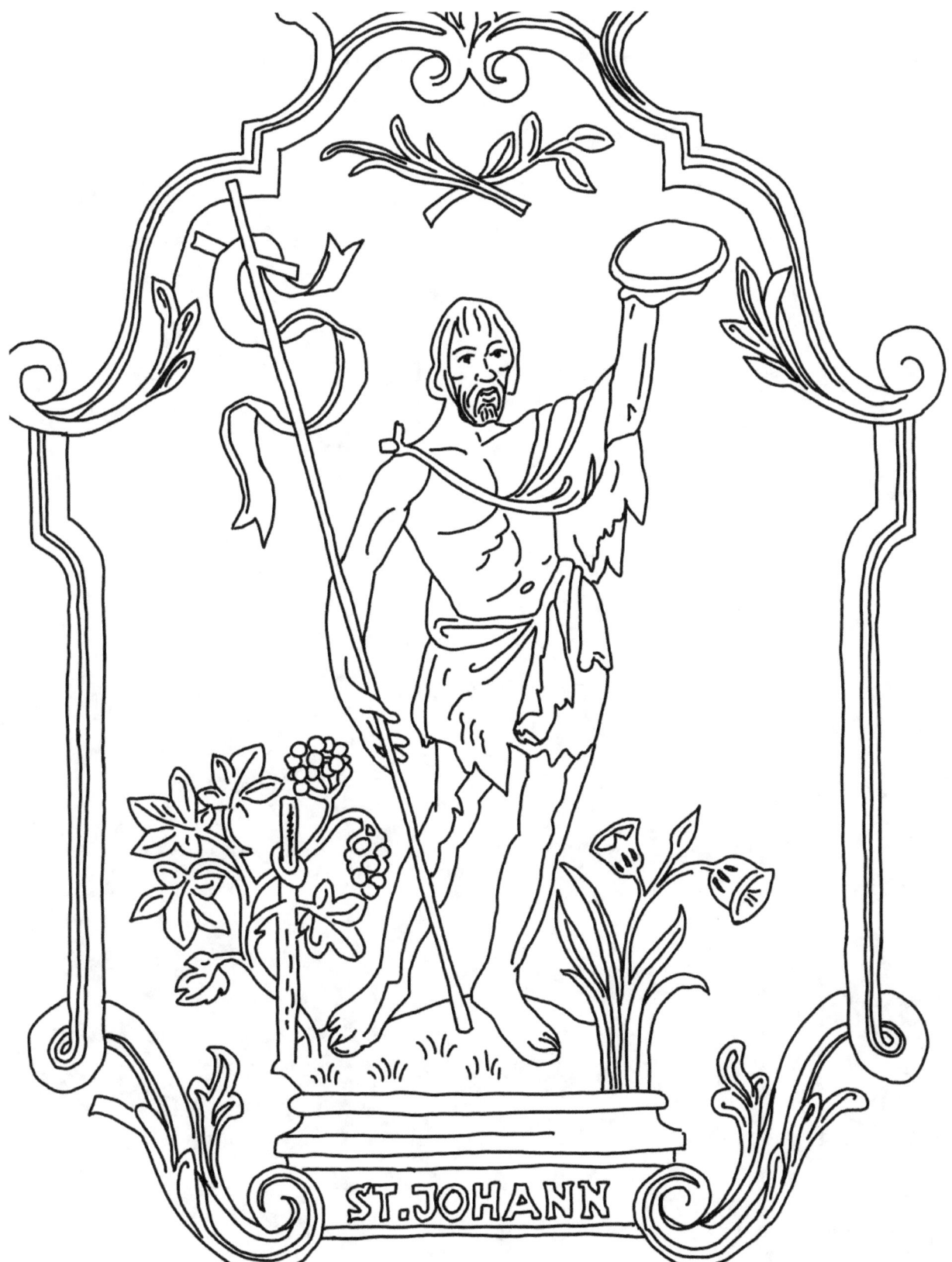

The old Maier Fabric House, Ludwigstraße 83, sgraffito done by Heinrich Bickel in 1925.

Unlike the other murals on this street which were painted into the plaster on the outsides of the buildings, this image of Saint John the Baptist was done in *sgraffito* — an Italian word for a technique of layering plaster in contrasting colors, and then carving out the underlying layer to make the picture.

ABOUT THE BOOK

The author is a lapsed lawyer turned folk-art historian and writer living in Bavaria. Before moving to the foothills of the Alps, he had a very square job in one of those very square states out West: he was a lawyer in Colorado. Following in the footsteps of Franz Joseph Bronner, who, 100 years earlier, armed with a camera and a notebook, set out to catalogue every Lüftlmalerei in the area around Garmisch-Partenkirchen, Justin Vazquez has attempted to do the same.

While new Lüftlmalerei may have been painted since, nothing else has changed since 1908, when Bronner wrote in *Von Deutscher Sitt' und Art*: "What summer visitor or tourist would not have enjoyed the old, gracefully painted farmhouses, of which there are still a considerable number in our high mountains! […] If one of the foreigners were to satisfy his thirst for knowledge and inquire about the creators of these paintings, he would most likely not receive half a dozen correct answers per hundred questions. Most of the locals know little or nothing about the matter, and looking up chronicles or guides does not make you feel much better. Admittedly, this painting is an art that stands in the street, and in some respects resembles folk song; one delights in these creations – without much asking who conceived them, who made them, or who brought them first."

www.ingramcontent.com/pod-product-compliance
Lightning Source LLC
Chambersburg PA
CBHW081709220526

45466CB00009B/2930